Marzec

Ready... Set... ENGLISH!

225 Ready-to-Use Starter Activities
for Grades 6-12

SANDRA MCTAVISH

THE CENTER FOR APPLIED
RESEARCH IN EDUCATION
Paramus, New Jersey 07652

Library of Congress Cataloging-in-Publication Data

McTavish, Sandra.
Ready, set, English! : 225 ready-to-use starter activities for grades 6-12 / Sandra McTavish.
p. cm.
ISBN 0-13-041049-7
1. English language—Study and teaching (Secondary) 2. Education, Secondary—Activity programs. I. Title.
LB1631 .M396 2001
428'.0071'2—dc21 2001017328

Acquisitions Editor: *Connie Kallback*
Senior Production Editor: *Jacqueline Roulette*
Interior Design/Page Layout: *Dimitra Coroneos*

Printed in the United States of America

10 9 8 7 6 5 4 3 2 1

ISBN 0-13-0410497

THE CENTER FOR APPLIED RESEARCH IN EDUCATION
Paramus, New Jersey 07652

http://www.phdirect.com

DEDICATION

To my favorite teachers: Lee Shea, Michael Moore, Mom and Dad

ACKNOWLEDGMENTS

There are many people I wish to thank for their help in getting this project from an idea into a book. Thanks to Connie Kallback, my editor, and Winfield Huppuch, for passing my initial proposal along to Connie. Thanks to Jacqueline Roulette, Production Editor, and Dee Coroneos, Formatter, at Prentice Hall Direct who worked on this book. Also, a big thanks to my parents, who looked at every word on every page. Thanks to Steve Salt for his help with the graphics. Special thanks go out to Doug Reid, Ian McTavish, Todd McTavish, Marni Martin, Sue Salt, Karen Salt, and Alison Reading for all their words of encouragement. Finally, I want to thank all my former students from Guelph Collegiate Institute, Centennial Collegiate Institute, Southwood Secondary School, Conestoga College, and Humber College for testing the material from this book.

ABOUT THE AUTHOR

Sandra McTavish earned an honors Bachelor of Arts in English literature from Wilfrid Laurier University in Waterloo, Ontario, and a Master of Science in Education from Canisius College in Buffalo, New York. She has five years' experience teaching on the intermediate and senior levels, and she currently is on leave from her position teaching English at Southwood Secondary School in Cambridge, Ontario, while she writes educational resource material at the Baxter Group and teaches English part-time at Humber College.

ABOUT THIS BOOK

Like most English teachers of grades 6–12, I have my own personal collection of resource books. Some of these books are full of spelling exercises, and others help me with the teaching of literature. Some focus on grammar, and others, on writing. What makes *Ready, Set, English!* particularly unique is that it touches on *all* the areas of study. The other benefit is that all the 225 activities are *ready-to-use,* which means all you have to do is photocopy them. Below is some information about what you will find in each section.

Literature—The worksheets in Section 1 can be used for the teaching of almost any short story, play, or novel. They cover a wide variety of topics that are examined in literature studies (e.g., the first line, setting, point of view, character development, plot development, conflict, symbolism, literary terms, etc.). Also, several of the worksheets help students identify authors and their works and learn about the history of American literature. These worksheets also work well with independent novel studies. Packages can be put together with various worksheets that students may be required to complete after reading their independent novel.

Writing—Section 2 begins with worksheets that examine the beauty of words, the structure of sentences, and stylistic devices. Here you'll find unique worksheets that encourage students to develop a love of writing poetry and help a writer when writing longer creative pieces. In addition, some worksheets will help students when writing dialogue, others help in the development of character, and others are simply intended to stimulate the creative juices. This section also teaches students how to write advertising slogans, a newspaper story, and thesis statements.

Reading—Section 3 focuses on reading comprehension and understanding. However, rather than have students read traditional stories, they will read e-mails, daytimers, classified ads, maps, newspaper stories, letters, and ad copy, and then answer questions. Other exercises allow students to follow instructions, follow a dialogue, and understand the meaning behind famous quotations. Finally, some worksheets look at how a story has changed over time and how changing an ending can alter the meaning behind an entire poem.

Grammar, Punctuation, and Sentence Structure—The focus of Section 4 is reinforcing grammar, punctuation, and other sentence structure issues in a way that's fun through the use of poems, puzzles, and games. The beginning features parts of speech, different types of nouns, and problems with verb tense. The section also addresses basic sentence problems, such as sentence fragments and run-on sentences. Other exercises reinforce the differences between subjects and objects, the differences between phrases and clauses, traditional problems with punctuation, capital letters, misplaced modifiers, homophones, irregular plurals, and the apostrophe.

Spelling—The worksheets in Section 5 help students learn to spell commonly misspelled words. In fact, all of the misspelled words are taken from a list of words that are commonly misspelled by middle and high school students. There are also some exercises to reinforce the spelling of the states, major American companies, and food. The section concludes with some fun enrichment spelling activities.

Vocabulary and Word Building—The worksheets in Section 6 provide a variety of different exercises that challenge students and help them improve and expand their vocabulary.

Listening and Speaking Skills—Listening and speaking skills are probably two of the most important skills a person needs in the world of work. The exercises in Section 7 allow students to fine-tune these important skills.

Word Fun—On a Friday afternoon or a rainy day when you are looking for an enrichment activity to occupy your very active students, you may want to use these activities from Section 8. Your students will find these exercises challenging, educational, and FUN!

You'll find this resource helpful and easy to use. So, let's get ready, set, and go!!

Sandra McTavish

CONTENTS

Section 1
LITERATURE

1. Judging a Book by Its Cover *2*
2. First Lines *3*
3. The Eight Components of a Story *4*
4. The Novel's Report Card *5*
5. The Mountain Climb: Examining Plot Structure *6*
6. Plot Fishing *7*
7. Mini Genres *8*
8. Conflicts *9*
9. Symbols and Symbolism *10*
10. The Setting and How It Can Affect the Story and Its Conflict *11*
11. A Setting Travel Ad *12*
12. Today versus Yesterday *13*
13. Looking at Point of View *14*
14. Comparing Characters *15*
15. The Journey *16*
16. Parent Figures *17*
17. Friends Are Friends Forever *18*
18. Pick a Career *19*
19. A Knapsack Character *20*
20. What Are People Saying? *21*
21. The Marketing Executive *22*
22. The High School Yearbook *23*
23. If I Won a Million Dollars *24*
24. A Look at Themes *25*
25. Compare and Contrast *26*
26. Changing the Ending *27*
27. The Movie versus the Book: The Great Debate *28*
28. If . . . *29*
29. Magic Squares: Literary Terms *30*
30. Timeline: A History of American Literature *31*

31. American Novelists and Their Novels *32*
32. Name That Author *33*
33. Famous English-Speaking Authors from Around the World *34*
34. Funny Titles *35*

Section 2
WRITING

35. A Few of Your Favorite Words *38*
36. Occupation Jargon Lists *39*
37. Sentence Construction *40*
38. Show, Don't Tell *41*
39. Clichés *42*
40. Stylistic Devices: Hyperbole and Personification *43*
41. Stylistic Devices: Similes and Metaphors *44*
42. The Me Poem *45*
43. Five Senses Poetry *46*
44. A Patchwork Quilt of Poetry *47*
45. A Group Poem *48*
46. Onomatopoeia *49*
47. An Acrostic Poem *50*
48. Word Painting *51*
49. Chance Poetry *52*
50. Story Fill-in *53*
51. What's in a Name *54*
52. Creating a Character *55*
53. The Interview *56*
54. And Then You Said . . . *57*
55. Opposites Converse *58*
56. Agony Ann Letters *59*
57. Word Adding *60*
58. Extend-a-Story *61*
59. Write the Beginning *63*
60. Finish the Story *64*
61. Knowing Your Audience *65*

62. A Warm Fuzzy *66*
63. Where Will I Be Ten Years from Today? *67*
64. Advertising Slogans *68*
65. Writing a Newspaper Story *69*
66. Writing a Good Thesis Statement *70*

Section 3
READING

67. Essay Introductions *72*
68. Answering the Famous Five *73*
69. Subjective or Objective *74*
70. Putting the News Story in Order *75*
71. Todd's Wig *76*
72. Dear Mr. Twain *78*
73. A Letter *79*
74. Picnic Insects *80*
75. Reading Ad Copy *81*
76. E-mails *83*
77. Ingrid's Daytimer *84*
78. Classifieds *85*
79. Subway Mania *86*
80. The Logic Puzzle *87*
81. Traditional versus Modern *88*
82. Reading Poetry *90*
83. Evaluating Endings *91*
84. Dialogue *92*
85. What Are They Doing? *93*
86. What Is Being Described? *94*
87. What Type of Story Is This? *95*
88. Describe the Shopper *96*
89. Directions *97*
90. What Are They Saying? 98
91. More of What They Are Saying *99*
92. A One-Minute Mystery *100*

Section 4
GRAMMAR, PUNCTUATION, AND SENTENCE STRUCTURE

93. Parts-of-Speech Poem *102*
94. Parts of Speech: Analogies *103*
95. Types of Nouns *104*
96. Collective Nouns *105*
97. Pronoun Fun *106*
98. Pronoun Problems *107*
99. Verb Tense *108*
100. More on Verbs *109*
101. Irregular Verb Forms *110*
102. Nouns, Adjectives, and Verbs *111*
103. Finding Subjects and Verbs *112*
104. Subject–Verb Agreement *113*
105. A Sentence or Not a Sentence *114*
106. Book Titles and Sentence Fragments *115*
107. Running Away with Run-On Sentences *116*
108. Do-It-Yourself Sentences *117*
109. Subjects, Predicates, and Objects *118*
110. More on Subjects, Predicates, and Objects *119*
111. Phrases, Clauses, and Conjunctions *120*
112. More on Phrases, Clauses, and Conjunctions *121*
113. Types of Sentences *122*
114. More About the Types of Sentences *123*
115. Parallelism *124*
116. Misplaced Modifiers *125*
117. Capitalization *126*
118. Homophones *127*
119. A Homophone Crossword *128*
120. Learning the Rules for Plurals *129*
121. Irregular Plurals *130*
122. The Apostrophe: Contraction *131*
123. The Apostrophe: Possession *132*
124. Quotation Marks *133*
125. Punctuation Puzzle *134*

126. Punctuation Dot-to-Dot *135*
127. Punctuation Multiple-Choice *136*
128. You're the Editor *137*

SECTION 5
SPELLING

129. Able or Ible *140*
130. Adding the Correct Letters *141*
131. What Is the Missing Vowel? *142*
132. Computer Cards and Your Spelling Errors *143*
133. Problem Words *144*
134. The Spelling Crossword *145*
135. The Spelling Bee *146*
136. Spelling Activity *147*
137. Spelling Demons *148*
138. Which One Belongs? *149*
139. Spelling Maze I *150*
140. Spelling Maze II *151*
141. Dot-to-Dot Spelling *152*
142. The Canadian Way *153*
143. The Menu *154*
144. The Job Application *155*
145. Spelling States *156*
146. A+ Spelling *157*
147. B+ Spelling *158*
148. The Spelling Hexagon *159*
149. The Spelling Box *160*

SECTION 6
VOCABULARY AND WORD BUILDING

150. Denotation and Connotation *162*
151. Word Wheels *163*
152. Four-Letter Word Fun *164*
153. Rhyming Wheels *165*

154. Creating "Sub" Words *166*
155. Creating "Port" Words *167*
156. Word Pyramids *168*
157. Magic Squares: E Words *169*
158. Improve Your Vocabulary *170*
159. Multiple-Choice Vocabulary *171*
160. Other Words *172*
161. A Letter *173*
162. An Antonym Box *174*
163. Another Antonym Box *175*
164. The Synonym Chart *176*
165. A Synonym Box *177*
166. Another Synonym Box *178*
167. Career Jargon *179*
168. Ology Vocabulary *180*
169. What Do They Fear? *181*
170. Which Word Doesn't Belong? (Part I) *182*
171. Which Word Doesn't Belong? (Part II) *183*
172. Which Word Doesn't Belong? (Part III) *184*

SECTION 7
LISTENING AND SPEAKING SKILLS

173. First-Day Bingo *186*
174. The Interview *187*
175. Great Speech Openings *188*
176. First Letter/Last Letter *189*
177. Evaluating Your Presentation and Public-Speaking Skills *190*
178. You Be the Judge *191*
179. The Survival Game *192*
180. New World Adventure *193*
181. Agree/Disagree/Undecided *194*
182. The 30-Second Practice *195*
183. Time Capsule *196*
184. Modified Telephone *197*
185. How Many Uses for an Object? *198*

186. Communication Exercise *199*
187. Charades *200*
188. Listening Skills Quiz *201*
189. The Substitute Teacher's Day *202*
190. The Shopping Trip *204*
191. The Listening Grid *206*
192. What's Missing? *208*
193. A Listening Poem *210*

Section 8
WORD FUN

194. Which Letter Comes Next? *214*
195. Simon Says *215*
196. A Simile Snake *216*
197. A Palindrome Letter *217*
198. Word Chains *218*
199. It Takes Three *219*
200. Career Alphabet *220*
201. Word Removal *221*
202. Analogies *222*
203. School Scramble *223*
204. Word Building *224*
205. Alphabet Soup *225*
206. Word Changes *226*
207. Unsolved Mysteries *227*
208. Rhyming Pairs *228*
209. What Is the Mystery Word? *229*
210. Letter Math *230*
211. Another Word Removal *231*
212. Going on a Camping Trip *232*
213. What's the Word? *233*
214. Letter Pairs *234*
215. More Alphabet Soup *235*
216. More Analogies *236*
217. Scrabble *237*

218. Circle Words *238*
219. More of Which Letter Comes Next? *239*
220. Simon Says Some More *240*
221. It Takes Three Again *241*
222. Person, Place, or Thing *242*
223. The Code *243*
224. More Word Changes *244*
225. More Rhyming Pairs *245*

ANSWER KEY *247*

Section 1

LITERATURE

*"Literature is both my joy and my comfort:
it can add to every happiness and there is no sorrow
it cannot console."*

PLING THE YOUNGER

Name ______________________________ Date ____________________

1. Judging a Book by Its Cover

(A Pre-Reading Activity)

Look at the cover of your book. Although there is a saying that tells us not to judge a book by its cover, covers, nevertheless, reveal much about the nature of the book. Examine the cover of your book as you answer the following questions.

Title of book: ____

1. Describe the cover of the book.

____

____

____

2. How does the cover make the book appeal to you?

____

____

____

3. By examining the cover, what do you predict the book will be about?

____

____

____

4. What information on the cover indicates the age level or type of person who might enjoy such a book?

____

____

____

5. How many colors are used on the cover? Why do you think these colors were chosen?

____

____

____

6. What genre is this book? How does the cover reveal the genre?

____

____

____

Name ______________________________ Date ____________________

2. First Lines

The first sentence of a novel or short story should entice the reader to want to read more. First lines usually:

- Draw the reader into the setting.
- Reveal something about the main character(s).
- Dive into the action of the story.

Examine the first sentences below from three famous novels. Comment on how each line effectively entices the reader to read more. Then examine the first line from the story you are currently reading and comment on it.

1. ***"Whether I shall turn out to be the hero of my own life, or whether that station will be held by anybody else, these pages must show."***

   David Copperfield BY CHARLES DICKENS

   ____

   ____

   ____

2. ***"They shoot the white girl first. With the rest they can take their time. No need to hurry out here."***

   Paradise BY TONI MORRISON

   ____

   ____

   ____

3. ***"The tropical rain fell in drenching sheets, hammering the corrugated roof of the clinic building, roaring down the metal gutters, splashing on the ground in a torrent."***

   Jurassic Park BY MICHAEL CRICHTON

   ____

   ____

   ____

4. Title of book: ______________________________

   The first sentence of your story: ______________________________

   ____

   ____

   ____

   Your comments: ______________________________

   ____

   ____

Name ______________________________ Date ____________________

3. The Eight Components of a Story

In the chart below are the eight components of a short story. Fill in the chart with one or two sentences about each component in connection with the story you just read.

Title of Story: ____

Plot
Theme
Character
Setting
Conflict
Point of View
Symbols
Style/Tone & Language

Name ______________________________ Date ____________________

4. The Novel's Report Card

Give the novel you have just read an A, B, C, D, or F for the following topics. Write a brief comment to justify your mark.

Title of Book: ____

TOPIC	MARK	COMMENTS
Plot (Give the book a grade based on how much the plot appealed to you.)		
Setting (Give a grade based on how appropriate the setting was to the story.) a) LOCATION		
b) TIME		
Main Character #1 Name ____________________ (Give a grade based on how much this character appealed to you.)		
Ending (Give a grade based on how much the ending satisfied you.)		
Title (Give a grade based on the appropriateness of the title.)		
Theme and Main Idea (Give a grade based on how much you liked the theme or main idea of the novel.)		
Overall Mark (Give an overall mark based on how much you liked the book.)		

Name ______________________________ Date ________________

5. The Mountain Climb: Examining Plot Structure

In many stories, the plot of the novel takes the path of a mountain climber. They both begin at the base of the mountain with a reason to climb. In a story, this is the introduction: the initial conflict gives the protagonist a reason to move forward.

Next, the plot and mountain climber climb toward the top. In a story this is called the rising action: The protagonist meets obstacles that are a result of the initial conflict.

After climbing upwards, the story reaches the peak of the mountain known as the climax. This is the highest point of interest in the story and usually the moment when the protagonist faces the antagonist.

After the climax at the top of the mountain, the story and climber both head down the mountain. This section is known in the story as the falling action: the moment when problems and conflicts are resolved.

Finally, the story and climber reach the base of the mountain. This is called the resolution: the initial conflict is addressed for the last time.

Now that you understand the traditional plot structure, use the mountain diagram and fill in the five sections with reference to the structure of the story you have just read.

Title of Story: ______________________________

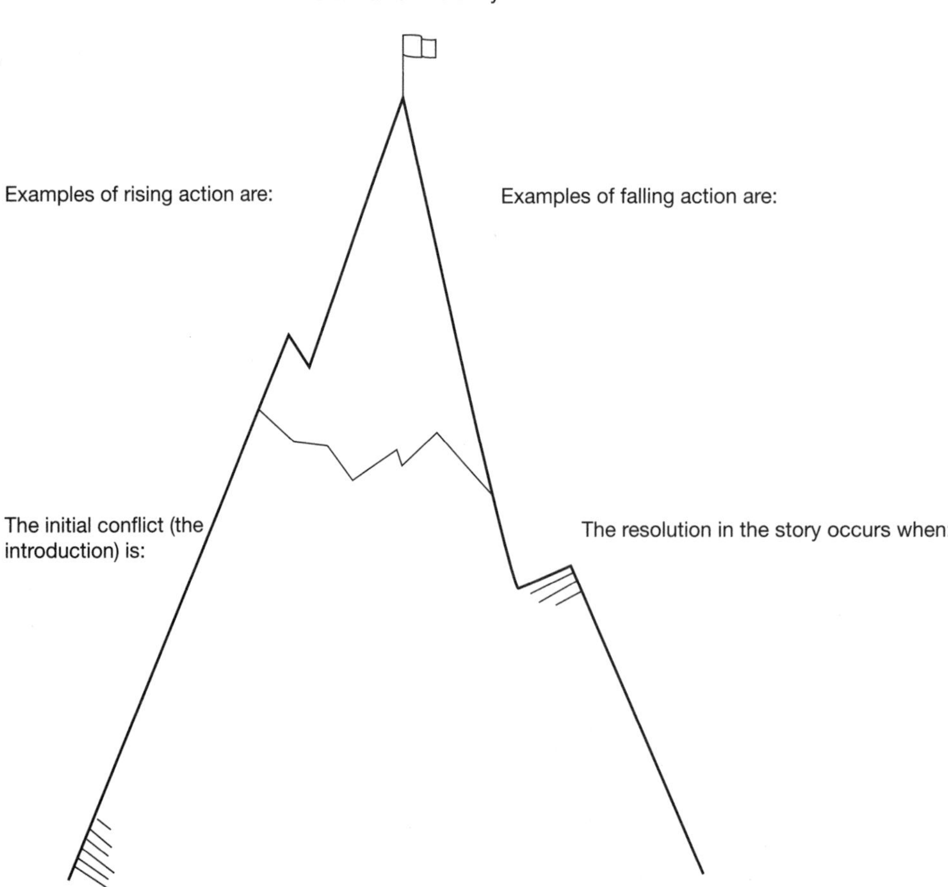
The climax of the story is:
Examples of rising action are:
Examples of falling action are:
The initial conflict (the introduction) is:
The resolution in the story occurs when:

Name ______________________________ Date ____________________

6. Plot Fishing

Most stories have dramatic points of interest that keep the reader interested. Below is a fishbone chart. Complete the chart by writing a few words on each "bone" indicating a dramatic point of the plot. Fill it out in the order the points occur in the story.

Title of Book: ____

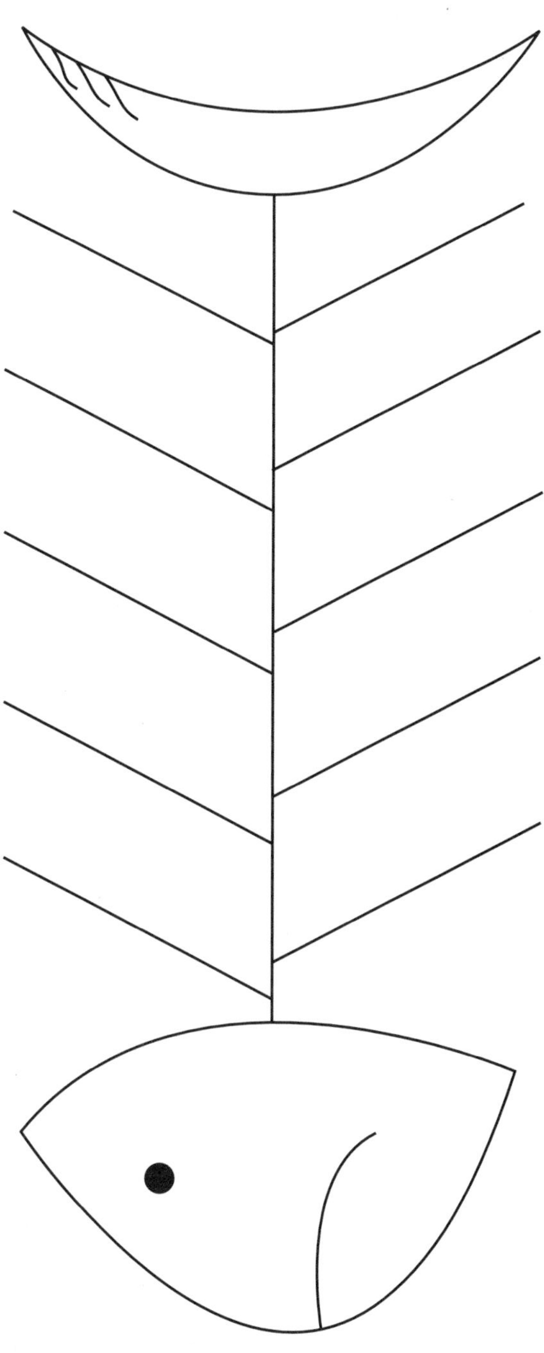

Name ______________________________ Date ______________

7. Mini Genres

Genre is "a literary type or class." Most books are usually categorized under one particular genre. However, they often include elements from other genres as well. For instance, a novel might be considered a comedy, but it might also have a romantic element. A number of genres are listed on the left-hand side in the chart below. In the right-hand column, give as many examples as possible of the genres from the book you are reading.

Title of Book: ______________________________

GENRES	EXAMPLE FROM YOUR BOOK
Drama	
Mystery	
Adventure	
Romance	
Comedy	
Science Fiction	

Name ______________________________ Date ________________

8. Conflicts

Good literature must include conflict. A book or a story is dull without conflict. Six types of conflicts often occur within a story. Examine the story you are currently reading and try to identify as many examples as possible for all the areas of conflict.

Title of Book: ____

TYPE OF CONFLICT	EXAMPLES
Person versus Person	
Person versus Him/Herself	
Person versus the Supernatural	
Person versus the Natural Environment	
Person versus a Group or Society	
Person versus Tradition (or the past)	

Name ______________________________ Date ____________________

9. Symbols and Symbolism

Symbols are objects that represent something else. For example, a red light tells drivers to stop. A Thanksgiving dinner, for many Americans, symbolizes a time to be thankful and to appreciate family. What do the items below symbolize to you? For 6, 7, and 8, write three symbols from the book you are currently reading and what these symbols symbolize.

1. Statue of Liberty

____

____

2. A Newborn Baby

____

____

3. The Color Yellow

____

____

4. December

____

____

5. Rain

____

____

Title of Book: ______________________________

6. Symbol #1 from Your Book: ______________________________

____

____

7. Symbol #2 from Your Book: ______________________________

____

____

8. Symbol #3 from Your Book: ______________________________

____

____

Name ______________________ Date ______________

10. The Setting and How It Can Affect the Story and Its Conflict

The setting of a story is usually appropriate to the story and its conflict. For instance, the conflict between blacks and whites in Mark Twain's novel *The Adventures of Huckleberry Finn* is strengthened because the setting is the Deep South in the late 1880s. The story and its main conflict would be quite different if the setting was Alaska in the 21st century. Think of the story you are currently reading. Below is a list of settings and time periods. Imagine how the plot and the main conflict might change if the story took place in those places and time periods. Write your thoughts about these changes on the lines next to each setting and time period.

Title of Book: ______________________

1. *Setting:* Colonial America
   Time Period: late 1600s when the first settlers arrived at a new country

   ____

   ____

   ____

2. *Setting:* another planet or space station
   Time Period: 100 years from today

   ____

   ____

   ____

3. *Setting:* America's Deep South
   Time Period: during the civil rights movement (1960s)

   ____

   ____

   ____

4. *Setting:* the town, city, or village in which you live
   Time Period: today

   ____

   ____

   ____

5. *Setting:* a village somewhere in an exotic, foreign country (you pick the country)
   Time Period: 100 years ago

   ____

   ____

   ____

Name ______________________________ Date ______________

11. A Setting Travel Ad

Advertising agencies hire copywriters to compose the "writing" part of ads. Pretend that you are a copywriter for an advertising agency in New York. Your company has been hired to create ads that will be published in travel magazines encouraging people to visit where the story you are reading takes place. Your job is to write persuasive and exciting copy that will accompany the visually appealing ad. In the space below, write the copy for the ad and indicate the type of pictures you think should be included. You may want to actually draw these pictures.

Title of Book: ______________________________

Name ______________________________ Date ____________________

12. Today versus Yesterday

Many of the books studied in school were written long before you were born. They were written before the Internet, airplanes, and the modern conveniences that we use today. How would the book you recently read be different if it had been written in today's world?

Title of Book: ____

1. How would the setting change if the book had been written today?

____

____

____

____

2. How would the main characters be different if they were living in today's world?

____

____

____

____

3. What aspects of the story would change if the book had been written today?

____

____

____

____

4. How would the main conflict change if the book had been written today?

____

____

____

____

5. How would the ending change if the book had been written today?

____

____

____

____

Name ______________________ Date ______________

13. Looking at Point of View

Point of view is the perspective from which a story is told. Sometimes a story is written in the first-person narrative, and the point of view is given entirely from that person's perspective. Or the story may be told from the perspective of a single character who is an observer or participant in the action; in this case, the author may write from a third-person narrative. Finally, the author may create an omniscient narrator. The word *omniscient* means "all-knowing or knows everything." This method enables the writer to present the inner thoughts and feelings of many characters.

Title of Book: ______________________

From what point of view is the story written?

____

____

____

Give evidence to prove that this is the point of view.

____

____

____

____

Why do you think the author chose to write this story from this particular point of view?

____

____

____

____

____

____

How would the story be different if it had been written from a different point of view?

____

____

____

____

____

____

Name ______________________________ Date ________________

14. Comparing Characters

Below is a list of common personality traits. Choose three of the traits from the list and write one in each of the three boxes labeled personality traits. Then choose two characters from the work you are currently reading. Put the names of those characters in the two appropriate boxes. Complete the chart by citing examples of occasions when each of the two characters exhibits these traits.

Title of Book: ____

Personality Traits List

pessimistic	fearless	insecure	manipulative
optimistic	joyful	extravagant	caring
honest	indecisive	friendly	prejudiced
deceitful	arrogant	integrity	helpful
fearful	shy	confident	romantic

PERSONALITY TRAITS	CHARACTER #1 NAME: ____________	CHARACTER #2 NAME: ____________
Trait #1		
Trait #2		
Trait #3		

Name ______________________________ Date ________________

15. The Journey

Many novels and short stories describe a character's journey. Sometimes this is a physical journey, as in Huckleberry Finn's journey down the Mississippi River, or it can be an inward or emotional journey. This exercise examines one character's journey from the book you just read. In each box, note the stage of the character's journey and what he/she has learned at this point. (You may wish to add extra boxes if there aren't enough.)

Title of Book: ______________________________

Name of Character: ______________________________

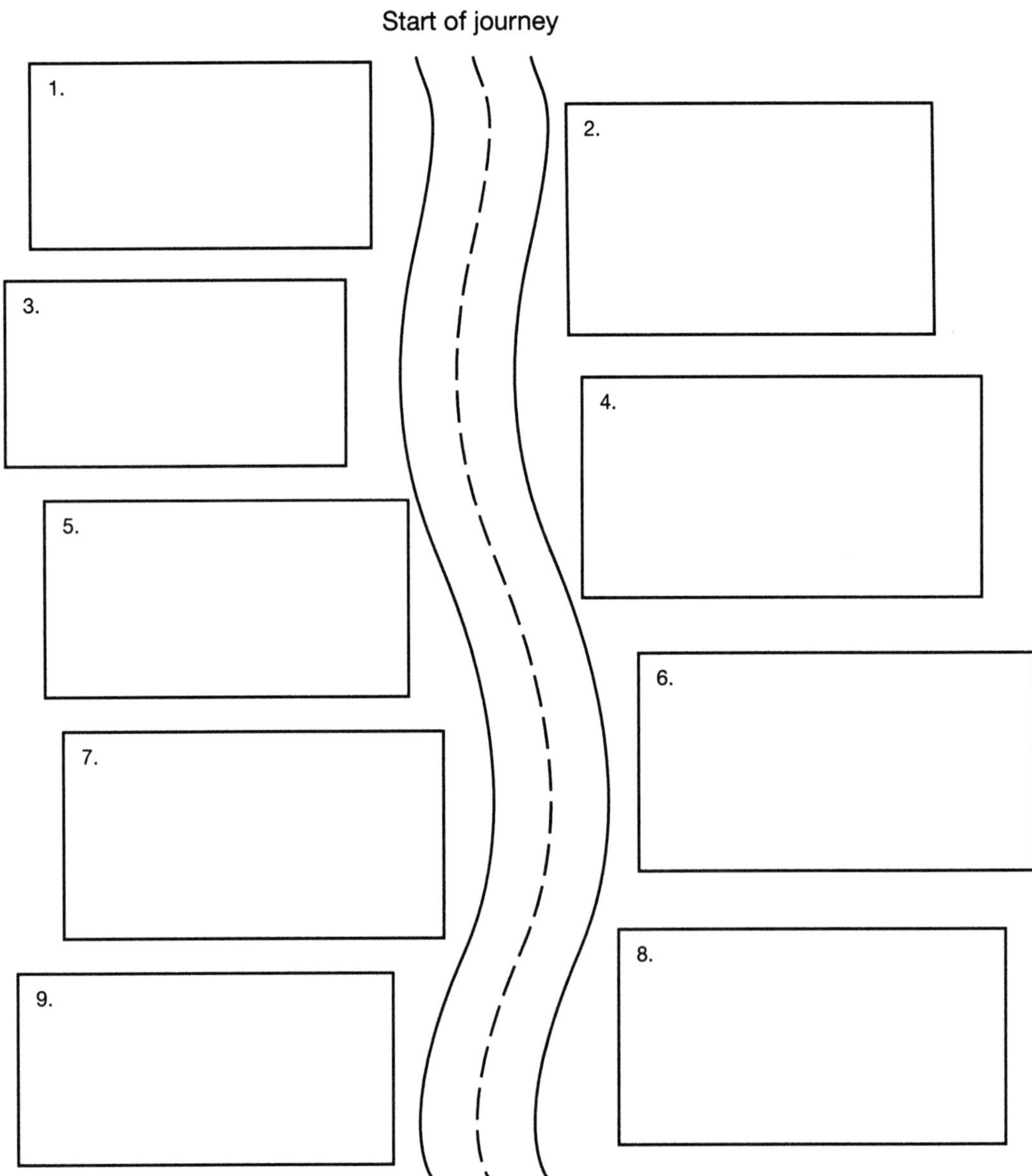

Name ______________________________ Date ______________

16. Parent Figures

In many novels, stories, and plays, various characters act as parents to younger characters. For example, in Harper Lee's novel *To Kill a Mockingbird,* Jem and Scout's mother has died leaving only their father, Atticus, as a parent. However, throughout the novel, others—such as Calpurnia, Aunt Alexandra, and Miss Maudie—assume the role of parent by giving Jem and Scout motherly advice and guidance.

Think of a young character in the story you are reading who receives parental guidance from various characters. Fill in the chart with the names of the three characters who provide such guidance. In the space in the center of the chart, provide specific examples from the book of the type of advice these characters give. Then, in the column on the far right, indicate how the main character receives this advice.

Title of Book: ______________________________

Name of young character who receives parental advice: ______________________________

NAME OF CHARACTERS WHO ARE LIKE PARENT-FIGURES	EXAMPLES OF THE ADVICE THEY OFFER	HOW THIS ADVICE IS RECEIVED BY THE CHARACTER
Character #1		
Character #2		
Character #3		

Name ______________________________ Date ____________________

17. Friends Are Friends Forever

Friends are important throughout our lives; they help shape us as human beings. Novels, stories, and plays often deal with friendships. Choose a character in the story you are currently reading who has many friends and then answer the questions below in connection with that character.

Title of Book: ______________________________

Name of character: ______________________________

1. Does this character have a best friend in the story? If so, who is it and what makes them best friends?

____

____

____

____

2. Does this character have a friend who betrays him/her and becomes an enemy in the end? Who is this betrayer and how does he/she betray your character?

____

____

____

____

3. Does this character have a friend who gets the character out of a difficult situation? Who is this friend and how does this friend help?

____

____

____

____

4. Does this character have a friend whose friendship is unexpected? Who is this friend and what makes their friendship so surprising?

____

____

____

____

5. Does this character have a friend who is so close that he/she is almost like family? Who is this character?

____

____

Name ______________________________ Date ______________

18. Pick a Career

Think of the book, short story, or play that you just finished reading. Imagine you bumped into the characters from the story a few years after it took place. Imagine also that the characters have either entered into a career for the first time or changed careers. Knowing what you know about each character, match each character with one of the following professions. Be prepared to explain why you think the character would enter the profession you have chosen.

Title of Book: ______________________________

Which character might become a . . .

SCIENTIST ______________________________

NURSE ______________________________

PROFESSIONAL ATHLETE ______________________________

CLOWN IN THE CIRCUS ______________________________

CHEF ______________________________

JUDGE ______________________________

POLITICIAN ______________________________

JOURNALIST ______________________________

PILOT ______________________________

WAITRESS OR WAITER ______________________________

TEACHER ______________________________

RELIGIOUS LEADER ______________________________

Name ______________________________ Date ____________________

19. A Knapsack Character

The L.A. Police Department found a knapsack. Below is a list of its contents. Write a description of the knapsack owner based on the contents of the knapsack.

1. a pair of binoculars
2. a baseball glove
3. suntan lotion
4. a copy of *Sports Illustrated*
5. a blank notebook
6. 4 pens
7. 3 chocolate bars
8. 2 bags of peanuts
9. 1 set of car keys
10. 6 pieces of LEGO

____

____

____

____

____

____

Now pick a character from a literary work that you are currently reading. Pick ten items this character might put in a knapsack and explain why he/she might have each item.

Title of Book: ____

____

____

____

____

____

____

____

____

____

____

____

____

____

____

Name ______________________________ Date ________________

20. What Are People Saying?

Imagine that the main character of the story you are reading met a psychiatrist. What would the psychiatrist say about that character? What would other professionals say about the character? Explain why they might think that way.

Title of Book: ______________________________

Name of Character: ______________________________

What would a **psychiatrist** say about this character? ______________________________

____

____

Why? ______________________________

____

What would a **spiritual leader** say about this character? ______________________________

____

____

Why? ______________________________

____

What would a **teacher** say about this character? ______________________________

____

____

Why? ______________________________

____

What would a **doctor** say about this character? ______________________________

____

____

Why? ______________________________

____

What would a **police officer** say about this character? ______________________________

____

____

Why? ______________________________

____

Name ______________________________ Date ______________

21. The Marketing Executive

People in marketing and advertising know that certain people and personality types buy certain products. Teenagers, for instance, are more likely than grandmothers to buy designer jeans. Pretend you are a marketing executive. For each product listed below, indicate the character, from a book you have recently read, who is most likely to buy the product.

Title of Book: ______________________________

1. Product: a brand new Porsche
   Character most likely to buy this product: ______________________________
   Why? ______________________________
   ____

2. Product: a day-timer and organizer
   Character most likely to buy this product: ______________________________
   Why? ______________________________
   ____

3. Product: a pair of running shoes
   Character most likely to buy this product: ______________________________
   Why? ______________________________
   ____

4. Product: a Harley Davidson motorcycle
   Character most likely to buy this product: ______________________________
   Why? ______________________________
   ____

5. Product: a hammer and nails
   Character most likely to buy this product: ______________________________
   Why? ______________________________
   ____

6. Product: four tickets to a Broadway play
   Character most likely to buy this product: ______________________________
   Why? ______________________________
   ____

Name ______________________________ Date ________________

22. The High School Yearbook

Imagine the characters from the book you are currently reading all attended the same high school. Pretend this is one of the pages from their high school yearbook. Choose characters from your book who might suit each of the following categories.

Title of Book: ______________________________

1. Most likely to become President of the United States.

____

2. Most likely to become a millionaire by age 30.

____

3. Most likely to win the Miss America beauty pageant.

____

4. Most likely to have grandchildren before anyone else in the graduating class.

____

5. Most likely to write a novel.

____

6. Most likely to win an Olympic gold medal.

____

7. Most likely to live on a bench in Central Park.

____

8. Most likely to save a drowning fish.

____

9. Most likely to move to Mars.

____

10. Most likely to need a psychiatrist.

____

Name ______________________________ Date ____________________

23. If I Won a Million Dollars

What would you do if you won a million dollars? Now think about three characters from the story you are reading. How would each of these characters spend a million dollars? Be prepared to explain to your classmates why you think each character would spend the money in the manner you have chosen. How does the character's personality determine his/her spending habits?

Title of Book: ______________________________

1. Character's Name: ______________________________

   What would this character do if he/she won a million dollars?

   ____
   ____
   ____
   ____
   ____
   ____
   ____

2. Character's Name: ______________________________

   What would this character do if he/she won a million dollars?

   ____
   ____
   ____
   ____
   ____
   ____
   ____

3. Character's Name: ______________________________

   What would this character do if he/she won a million dollars?

   ____
   ____
   ____
   ____
   ____
   ____
   ____

Name ______________________________ Date ______________

24. A Look at Themes

The theme of a work is its main idea or thesis. The theme may be directly or indirectly stated. There are some universal themes that often appear in literary works. The chart below lists some of these universal themes. In the Rating box, put a number between 1–3: 1 means this theme is the key theme in the story you are reading; 2 means this theme is part of the story, but it is not the main theme of the story; 3 means this theme is not mentioned in the story. In the comments column, indicate in a sentence or two how this theme is developed in the story.

Title of Book: ______________________________

RATING	THEME	COMMENTS
	An attempt by the protagonist (or a group) to attain the American Dream	
	The blurred boundaries of appearance versus reality	
	The problems that occur when an individual or a group abuses power	
	The realization that love conquers all	
	The survival of the fittest	
	An attempt to challenge and change the views of a society or group	
	Dealing with the problems that occur when one is coming of age and entering the adult world	
	A personal and spiritual quest for happiness and purpose in life	
	Learning the difference between good and evil	
	A realization that art lasts forever, but life does not	

Name ______________________________ Date ______________

25. Compare and Contrast

Often two stories may have some similarities and a number of differences. Use the chart below to examine the similarities and differences between two stories, plays, poems, or novels you are studying. Where the two diamonds join, note the similarities between the two works. Where the diamonds are separate, note the differences in each story. You may wish to examine the similarities or differences in plot, character, setting, conflict, point of view, etc.

Title for story 1: ______________________

Title for story 2: ______________________

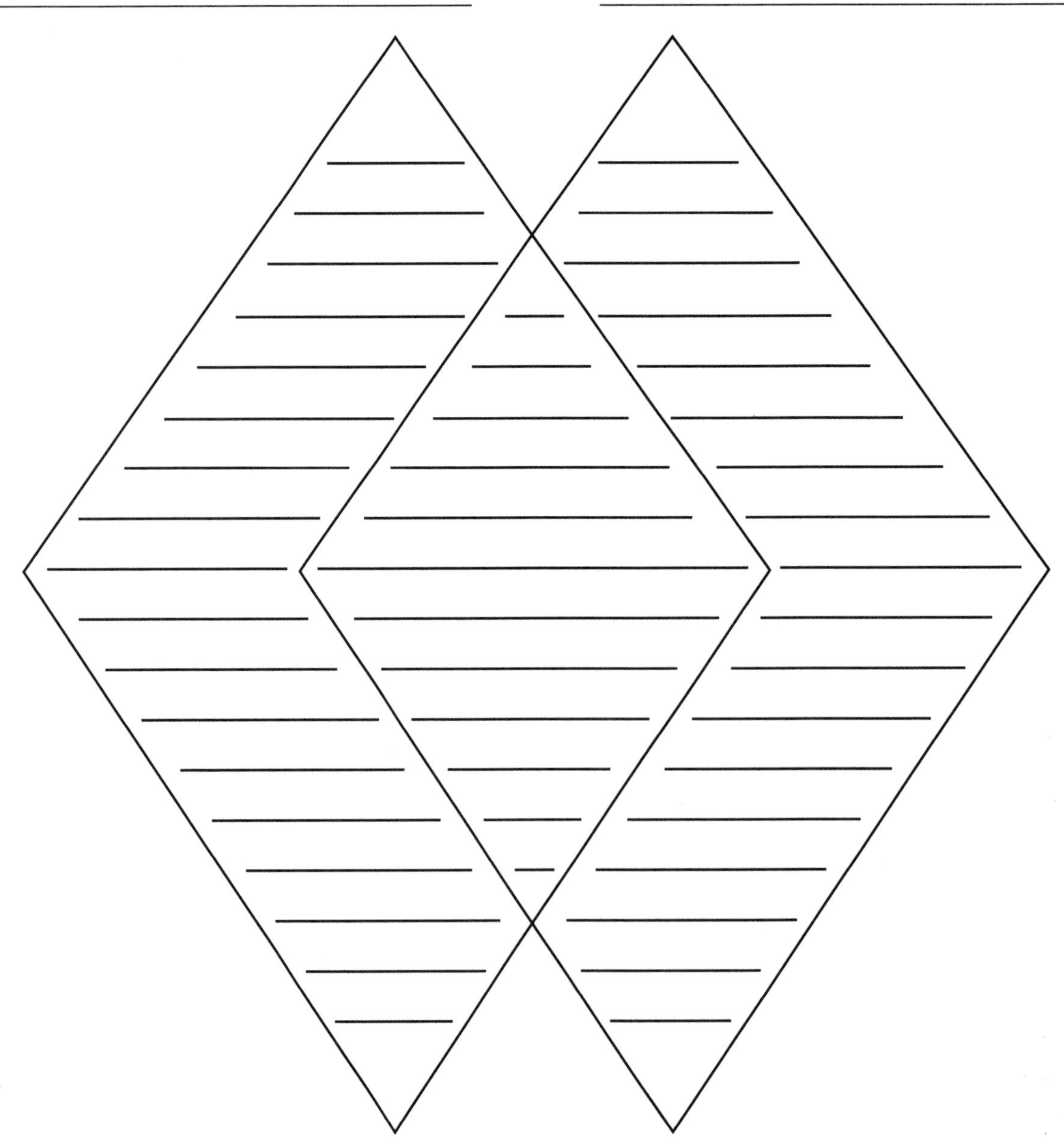

Name ______________________________ Date ____________________

26. Changing the Ending

Many people finish a book and have other ideas about how it should have ended. Consider the story you have just read. How might its ending be different? In the space below, compose a different version of the story's ending.

Title of Book: ______________________________

Name ______________________________ Date ________________

27. The Movie versus the Book: the Great Debate

Many books or plays have film versions. Naturally it is difficult to squeeze all the action of a lengthy book or play into a two-hour movie. Thus, it is rare for any film to remain completely faithful to the book. After reading the book, watch the movie version and answer the questions below.

Title of Book: ______________________________

Title of Movie: ______________________________

1. What parts of the book did the movie version leave out? Why do you think these parts were left out?

____

____

____

____

2. Were there any parts in the film that were added and not part of the original story? Why do you think they were added?

____

____

3. What was your favorite part in the movie? Why?

____

____

4. What was your favorite part in the book? Why?

____

____

5. If you could make any changes to the film, what would they be? Why?

____

____

____

6. Which did you like more: the movie or the book? Why?

____

____

____

Name ______________________________ Date ______________

28. If . . .

Think of the settings and characters from all the books you have read. Now pick characters and a setting that allow you to answer the following questions.

1. If you could marry a literary character, which one would it be?

   Character: ______________________________

   From the book: ______________________________

2. If you could become best friends with a literary character, which one would you choose?

   Character: ______________________________

   From the book: ______________________________

3. Of all the books you have read, which character would be your enemy if you met him/her?

   Character: ______________________________

   From the book: ______________________________

4.a. If you could pick your parents from a book you have read, who would you choose to be your mother?

   Character: ______________________________

   From the book: ______________________________

4.b. Who would be your father?

   Character: ______________________________

   From the book: ______________________________

5. Which literary character would you like to see interviewed on a talk show?

   Character: ______________________________

   From the book: ______________________________

6. If you became sick or unwell, which literary character would you want to take care of you?

   Character: ______________________________

   From the book: ______________________________

7. If you could move to a town or city from one of the books you have read, where would you want to live?

   Location: ______________________________

   From the book: ______________________________

Name ______________________________ Date ____________________

29. Magic Squares: Literary Terms

From the numbered statements, select the best answer for each literary term. Insert the number in the appropriate box of the magic square. The sum of the numbers in the box will be the same across each row and down each column. This sum is the magic number.

LITERARY TERMS	STATEMENTS
(A) ALLITERATION(2)	The repetition of consonant sounds
(B) ANALOGY	(3) The attribution of human characteristics to inanimate objects
(C) ASSONANCE	(4) A comparison of two unlike objects using "like" or "as"
(D) FORESHADOWING	(5) Descriptively representing a thing, actions, or ideas
(E) HYPERBOLE	(6) Words whose sounds express their meaning
(F) IMAGERY	(7) A resemblance between two different things
(G) IRONY	(8) Deliberate exaggeration
(H) MALAPROPISM	(9) A word or phrase representing abstract ideas
(I) METAPHOR	(10) The ridicule of a subject or idea
(J) OXYMORON	(11) An expression of meaning, opposite to the stated one
(K) ONOMATOPOEIA	(12) Clues to future events
(L) PERSONIFICATION	(13) A comparison of two unlike objects
(M) PUN	(15) A blunder in speech caused by word substitution
(N) SATIRE	(16) Word play involving words with different meaning but similar spelling
(O) SIMILE	(17) Two contradictory terms that express a paradox
(P) SYMBOL	(18) A repetition of similar vowel sounds, usually stressed in syllables

THE MAGIC SQUARE

A	B	C	D
E	F	G	H
I	J	K	L
M	N	O	P

THE MAGIC NUMBER IS ________

Name ______________________________ Date ____________________

30. Timeline: A History of American Literature

Here is a list of significant highlights in American literature. Arrange the events in the order in which they occurred by placing the number of the event on the timeline below. The first one is done for you.

1. The first Pulitzer Prizes are presented. (Pulitzer Prizes, created by great American journalist Joseph Pulitzer, are presented to Americans annually in such areas as literature, journalism, play writing, and poetry.)
2. *The Great Gatsby* by F. Scott Fitzgerald, considered by many to be the greatest American novel of all time, is first published.
3. Thomas Jefferson writes *The Declaration of Independence,* considered by many to be the most important piece of writing in America.
4. Toni Morrison, one of America's leading female writers, wins the Nobel Prize for Literature.
5. Phillis Wheatley, the first American black writer of consequence, becomes famous with her poem on the death of the Reverend George Whitfield.
6. *The Power of Sympathy* by William Hill Brown, considered the first American novel, is published.
7. Sinclair Lewis becomes the first American writer to win the Nobel Prize for Literature.
8. Ernest Hemingway, considered by many to be the greatest American writer of all time, is born.
9. Stephen King, referred to as "the world's most successful writer," publishes his first novel *Carrie.*

LEAST RECENT __5__ ____ ____ ____ ____ ____ ____ ____ ____ MOST RECENT

Name ______________________________________ Date ____________________

31. American Novelists and Their Novels

How well do you know American novelists and the novels they have written? Match the novelist from column A with one of the novels he/she has written in column B.

Column A	Column B
1. Ray Bradbury	____ *The Great Gatsby*
2. Joyce Carol Oates	____ *The Grapes of Wrath*
3. F. Scott Fitzgerald	____ *A Separate Peace*
4. Nathaniel Hawthorne	____ *The Catcher in the Rye*
5. Ernest Hemingway	____ *Fahrenheit 451*
6. John Irving	____ *Moby Dick*
7. Ken Kesey	____ *The Old Man and the Sea*
8. John Knowles	____ *One Flew Over the Cuckoo's Nest*
9. Herman Melville	____ *The Adventures of Tom Sawyer*
10. J. D. Salinger	____ *The Scarlet Letter*
11. John Steinbeck	____ *The Color Purple*
12. Amy Tan	____ *The Joy Luck Club*
13. Mark Twain	____ *Rabbit, Run*
14. John Updike	____ *The World According to Garp*
15. Alice Walker	____ *Them*

Name ______________________________ Date ________________

32. Name That Author

Use the clues in the chart to determine which American author is being described.

	AUTHOR #1	AUTHOR #2	AUTHOR #3
Year of birth	1835	1947	1830
Year of death	1910	still living	1886
Birthplace	Florida, Missouri	Portland, Maine	Amherst, Massachusetts
Education/jobs	Had a number of jobs: worked as a printer; worked on a Mississippi steamboat; journalist	Graduated from the University of Maine, then taught high school English for a short time	Spent one year at a female seminary and spent all her adult life living at home (never worked outside the home)
Marital status	Married Olivia Langdon; they had 3 daughters	Married Tabitha Spruce; they have 2 sons and 1 daughter	Never married
Additional information	His real name was Samuel Clemens	Many of his works have been made into movies	After the age of 30, she became a recluse and rarely saw people outside of her immediate family
Name of first publication	*The Celebrated Jumping Frog of Calaveras County* (1867)	*Carrie* (1973)	Only published a few of her poems in her lifetime. All of her books of poems (the first called *Poems)* were published posthumously.
Who is the author?			

Name ______________________________ Date ____________________

33. Famous English-Speaking Authors from Around the World

How well do you know who wrote what? Use the clues below to help fill in the crossword. (Use last names only.)

Across

2. She had *Pride and Prejudice* and *Sense and Sensibility.*
4. The creator of *Tom Sawyer.*
5. She found *The Secret Garden.*
6. He wrote *Death of a Salesman.*
8. This Canadian tells *A Handmaid's Tale.*
11. He had a *Heart of Darkness.*
12. This classic author is famous for his *Faerie Queen.*
14. She wrote *To Kill a Mockingbird.*
15. His play is *A Streetcar Named Desire.*
16. She created *Anne of Green Gables.*
18. He painted *The Picture of Dorian Gray.*
19. She gave us *Little Women.*

Down

1. He gave Hester Prynne her *Scarlet Letter.*
3. He's a *Catcher in the Rye.*
5. She wrote *Wuthering Heights* and her sister wrote *Jane Eyre.*
7. He gave life to *Tess of the D'urbervilles* and *Jude the Obscure.*
9. The author of *Animal Farm.*
10. He provided us with *Robinson Crusoe.*
12. He sent Gulliver on his travels in *Gulliver's Travels.*
13. He gave us *Romeo and Juliet.*
17. The author of *Oliver Twist.*

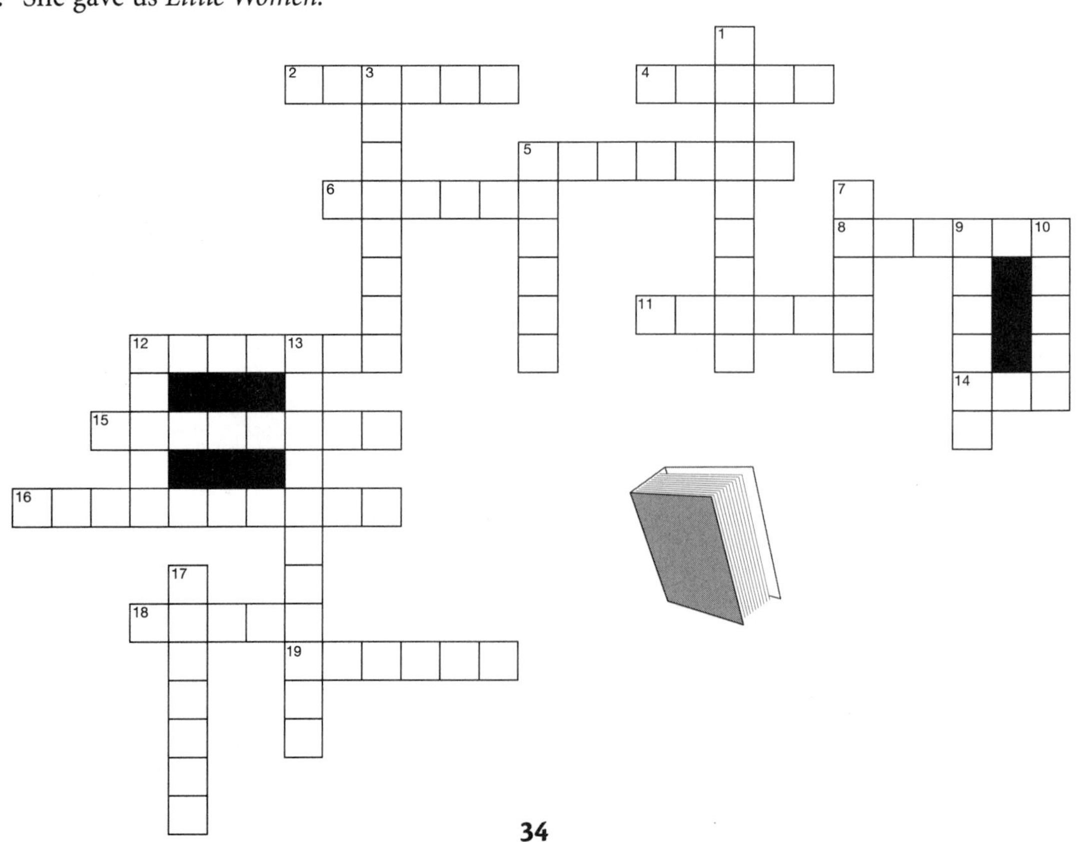

Name ______________________________ Date ________________

34. Funny Titles

Identify the titles of the classic novels, plays, and children's stories by using the clues in each box. The story in box A-1, for example, is a Dr. Seuss classic: *The Cat in the Hat.*

	A	B	C
1	**hcatat**	*night night night* *night night night* *night night night* *night night night*	the opposite of princess and the opposite of rich person
2	451 ^{0}F	PE ACE	**cat** **hot tin roof**
3	women	opposite of scared opposite of old [picture of a globe]	RcatcherYE
4	[picture of a house] cider another word for Laws	A Story of City City	[picture of grapes] of fierce anger

Section 2

WRITING

"If you wish to be a writer, write."

EPICTETUS

Name ______________________________ Date ____________________

35. A Few of Your Favorite Words

Writers love words. They love the way words sound as they are spoken; they love the way words look on the page. They also like words for what they mean. Many writers have lists of favorite words. Think of your own favorites. List them below.

1. ______________________ 20. ______________________
2. ______________________ 21. ______________________
3. ______________________ 22. ______________________
4. ______________________ 23. ______________________
5. ______________________ 24. ______________________
6. ______________________ 25. ______________________
7. ______________________ 26. ______________________
8. ______________________ 27. ______________________
9. ______________________ 28. ______________________
10. ______________________ 29. ______________________
11. ______________________ 30. ______________________
12. ______________________ 31. ______________________
13. ______________________ 32. ______________________
14. ______________________ 33. ______________________
15. ______________________ 34. ______________________
16. ______________________ 35. ______________________
17. ______________________ 36. ______________________
18. ______________________ 37. ______________________
19. ______________________ 38. ______________________

Name ______________________________ Date ____________________

36. Occupation Jargon Lists

A good writer develops characters and has them talk and act realistically. For example, if the writer has an astronaut in the story, the astronaut would use words that are common in his/her profession. Therefore, a good writer, when developing a character, must learn about the type of vocabulary this character would know and use. Listed below are some occupations. Make a list of words a person in that occupation might use. Try not to use simple words. *Helpful Hint:* You may wish to use a dictionary.

CHEF	GARDENER	PROFESSIONAL FOOTBALL COACH	PRESIDENT OF THE U.S.

DOCTOR	PILOT	DAIRY FARMER	VETERINARIAN

Name ______________________________ Date ______________

37. Sentence Construction

Good writers vary their sentence lengths. They do not, for example, only use short, simple sentences. Rewrite each group of simple sentences into one longer, complex sentence.

Group 1

Arlene has been skating since age three.
She loves figure skating.
Her favorite figure skater is Michelle Kwan.
Arlene wants to be just like Michelle Kwan.
Arlene wants to be in the Olympics.

Your Sentence

____

____

____

____

____

Group 2

Gerry lives in Chapel Hill, North Carolina.
His father works for a company called New Wave Technology.
His father's name is Bud.
His father's company transferred him.
The family will be moving to Alaska.
Gerry does not want to move.

Your Sentence

____

____

____

____

____

Name ______________________________ Date ____________________

38. Show, Don't Tell

New writers are often advised, "Show, don't tell." For example, telling us that "Carl is cheap and inconsiderate" is not nearly so effective as *showing* these characteristics in action by writing: "Carl went up to the beggar and asked if he could spare a quarter because Carl resented spending money on a pay phone." Each statement below *tells* about a character or a place. Write a statement that *shows* what the character is like. For example:

Tell—It is hot outside.

Show—It is so hot outside that I could have fried an egg on the sidewalk.

1. TELL—North Dakota experienced a cold winter.

   SHOW—______________________________

   ____

   ____

2. TELL—Zanida is hyper.

   SHOW—______________________________

   ____

   ____

3. TELL—The Magic Kingdom is busy.

   SHOW—______________________________

   ____

   ____

4. TELL—Mrs. Nguyen is scared of the neighbor's dog.

   SHOW—______________________________

   ____

   ____

5. TELL—Mr. Dhaliwal is rich.

   SHOW—______________________________

   ____

   ____

Name ______________________________ Date ____________________

39. Clichés

Clichés are phrases or expressions that have been repeated so often that they have become trite and hackneyed. Below are some common clichés. Rewrite each cliché to make it sound fresh and original without changing its meaning. Here is an example:

Cliché: He eats like a pig.
Rewording: He eats like a man who lives in a junkyard.

Now it's your turn.

Cliché: You can't have your cake and eat it too.

Rewording: ______________________________

____

Cliché: The grass is always greener on the other side.

Rewording: ______________________________

____

Cliché: Every cloud has a silver lining.

Rewording: ______________________________

____

Cliché: A picture is worth a thousand words.

Rewording: ______________________________

____

Cliché: His bark is worse than his bite.

Rewording: ______________________________

____

Cliché: Her head is in the clouds.

Rewording: ______________________________

____

Cliché: She is scared of her own shadow.

Rewording: ______________________________

____

Name ______________________________ Date ____________________

40. Stylistic Devices: Hyperbole and Personification

Stylistic devices are tools writers use to make their writing more colorful and memorable. The two stylistic devices we examine on this worksheet are hyperbole and personification.

Hyperbole

Definition: Hyperbole expresses an obvious exaggeration.

Example: She's dying to meet her favorite movie star.

Instructions: Finish each statement with an obvious exaggeration.

He bores me ______________________________

You make as much noise ______________________________

He ate so much ______________________________

She was so hyper that ______________________________

The concert was so wild that ______________________________

Personification

Definition: Personification attributes human characteristics to inanimate objects, animals, or ideas.

Example: The flowers bowed down to the rain.

Instructions: Write a sentence in which you personify each object or thing.

TIME ______________________________

____

PENS ______________________________

____

TREES ______________________________

____

EMPIRE STATE BUILDING ______________________________

____

BEACH ______________________________

____

Name ______________________________ Date ____________________

41. Stylistic Devices: Similes and Metaphors

Stylistic devices are tools writers use to make their writing more colorful and memorable. The two stylistic devices you will examine on this worksheet are similes and metaphors.

Similes

Definition: A simile is a comparison between two unlike things using *like* or *as.*
Example: She smelled like a rose.

Instructions: Complete the similes by filling in the blanks with a word or a phrase. Try to be as creative as you can.

As short as ______________________________

As blue as ______________________________

As fast as ______________________________

The sand was like ______________________________

The summer passed by like ______________________________

Metaphors

Definition: A metaphor is a comparison that states two different things are alike without using *like* or *as.*
Example: My used car is a nightmare.

Instructions: Use each word to create a metaphor.

(CLOCK) ______________________________

____

(USA) ______________________________

____

(COMPUTERS) ______________________________

____

(SCHOOL) ______________________________

____

(BIRTHDAYS) ______________________________

____

Name ______________________________ Date ________________

42. The Me Poem

Writing poetry may seem difficult; however, by following the formula below, you can easily write a poem. The topic is YOU! This will also allow your teacher to get to know you a little better.

The ME Poem Formula

Line 1	Your first name
Line 2	Who wants to become . . .
Line 3	Son/Daughter of . . .
Line 4	Three adjectives that describe you
Line 5	Three activities you enjoy doing
Line 6	Friends with (name three friends)
Line 7	Resident of (street and city/town)
Line 8	Last name

A Sample

Brooke
Who wants to become a doctor
Daughter of Hoi and Elizabeth
Friendly, optimistic, and busy
A reader, volleyball player, and a cellist
Friends with Bashil, Van, and Jennifer
Resident of Houston, Texas
Chang

Now it's your turn!

____

____

____

____

____

____

____

____

Name ______________________________ Date ____________________

43. Five Senses Poetry

When writing poetry, it is important to try to use as many of the five senses as possible. Imagine a fire. Use the word *orange* to describe what you see; *crackling* to describe what you hear; *hot* to describe what you feel; and *smoky* to describe what you smell. Put these four words together and here is your poem.

Fire

Orange
Smoky
Crackling
Hot
Fire

Make your own poem by thinking of a word for each of the five senses to describe a lake or an ocean.

SIGHT WORD ______________________________

SOUND WORD ______________________________

TASTE WORD ______________________________

TOUCH WORD ______________________________

SMELL WORD ______________________________

SUBJECT ______________________________

Create your own subject and find words from the five senses to describe that subject.

SIGHT WORD ______________________________

SOUND WORD ______________________________

TASTE WORD ______________________________

TOUCH WORD ______________________________

SMELL WORD ______________________________

SUBJECT ______________________________

44. A Patchwork Quilt of Poetry

A patchwork quilt is made up of leftover scraps of material. In this exercise, you will make a patchwork quilt poem. Listed below are lines from various great American poems. Use as many of these lines as you can in a single poem connecting these lines to lines of your own. You may use small portions of the lines provided, and you may wish to change the occasional word (or tense) of the lines. Try not to alter the lines too much. Good luck!

And now: it is easy to forget
What I came for.
Adrienne Rich, *"Diving into the Wreck"*

This hour I tell things in confidence,
I might not tell everybody, but I will tell you.
Walt Whitman, *"Song of Myself"*

Success is counted sweetest
By those who ne'er succeed.
Emily Dickinson, *"#67"*

My soul has grown deep like the rivers.
Langston Hughes, *"The Negro Speaks of Rivers"*

Two roads diverged in a wood, and I—
I took the one less traveled by,
And that has made all the difference."
Robert Frost, *"The Road not Taken"*

What place is this
Where are we now?
Carl Sandburg, *"Grass"*

And indeed there will be time
To wonder, 'Do I dare?' and, 'Do I dare?'
T.S. Eliot, *"The Love Song of J. Alfred Prufrock"*

It is a human love, I live inside
Imamu Amiri Baraka, *"An Agony as Now"*

A last look brings me
To the hills' northern face, and the face is orange rock
That looks out on nothing but a great space
Of white and pewter lights.
Sylvia Plath, *"Blackberrying"*

It was here. That was the setting and the time
Of year. Here in this house and in his room,
In his chair, the most tranquil thought peaked.
Wallace Stevens, *"A Quiet Normal Life"*

Take thought:
I have weathered the storm,
I have beaten out my exile.
Ezra Pound, *"The Rest"*

Name ______________________________ Date ________________

45. A Group Poem

A number of people will help write a poem in this exercise. Each person in the class will have a copy of this sheet. On it, you will contribute the first line of your poem. Then you will pass the paper to the person sitting behind you and that person will contribute the second line. Meanwhile, you will receive the paper from the person in front of you and will contribute the second line of that person's poem. This continues until the poems are finished. Make sure your name is on the top of your *original* page, so your poem gets returned to you when it is finished. The first person will establish the title of the poem.

Title: ______________________________

Line 1—Begin the poem with a simile.

____

____

Line 2—Refer to one of the five senses.

____

____

Line 3—Use three verbs.

____

____

Line 4—Use three adjectives and a noun.

____

____

Line 5—Create a line that uses personification.

____

____

Line 6—Create a line that uses hyperbole.

____

____

Line 7—Refer to a natural image.

____

____

Line 8—End the poem with a powerful last line.

____

____

Name ______________________________ Date ____________________

46. Onomatopoeia

Onomatopoeia is the term given to words borrowed from sounds. The words resemble the sounds to which they refer. Examples of such words are *honk, moo, rustle,* and *bang.* How many other onomatopoeic words can you think of? Write them on a separate sheet of paper.

Here is a description of an irritating bug:

BUZZ BUZZ BUZZ BUZZ SWAT!
BUZZ **BUZZ** **BUZZ**

Now it's your turn to try to use onomatopoeic words to describe the following situations:

1. A train rolling into a station

2. A leaky faucet that is not getting any better

3. A barnyard at sunrise

Name ______________________________ Date ____________________

47. An Acrostic Poem

Write your name from top to bottom on the left side of the page. Use each letter of your name as the first letter in a line of the poem. Have the poem describe you or your hopes and dreams. Here is a sample:

S itting on
A unt Florence's antique chair
N oticing the rain outside
D reaming about
R unning in the
A nawanda marathon.

Now it's your turn.

Name ______________________________ Date ____________________

48. Word Painting

A word painting combines words and art to create a pictorial image. Below is a word painting called "My Favorite Things." Using this illustrated concept as a guide, create a word painting of your favorite things in the space below.

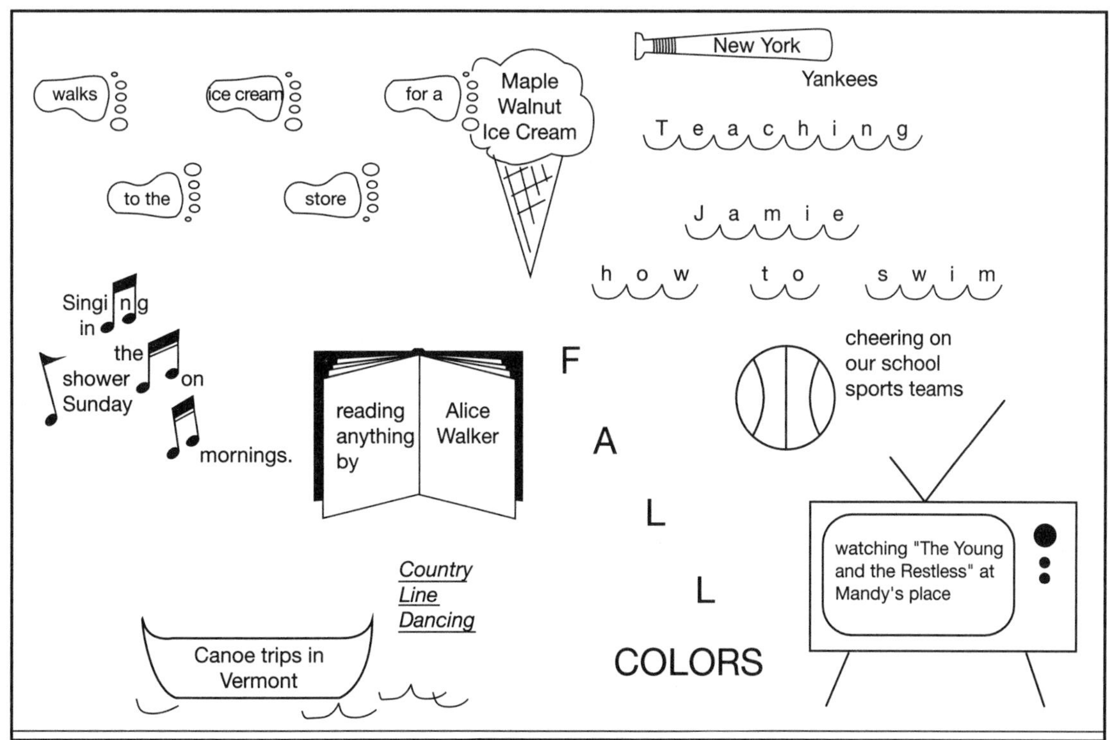

Name ______________________________ Date ____________________

49. Chance Poetry

The box shows a random selection of words. Pick some or all of the words from the box and create a poem. The poem may take any form or shape. Try not to use words that do not appear in the box. (You may, however, alter the verb tenses.)

Dance Two A The Concert Light Judge
Because Hide Run Want Harmony Around We Are Circle
I You Of Not Do Between Stand Maintain Relationship
Friendship One Up To In See With Cave Breeze Sun On
Coward Anger Rivers Earth Wish Need Therefore But Climb And Life
Just Mountain Cows Clowns Act Before Over Get Find Compete
Almost Never Teacup Marsh Green Friend Music Will Crack When
Can Down Absurdity Ever Know Hear Listen Ear Fringe Many Things
Me Palm Trees Car Sunset What If Or Hello Cry Need Fire

Name ________________________________ Date ________________

50. Story Fill-In

Fill in a word (or words) of your choice any time a blank appears. Make sure the chosen word makes sense in the story.

Late one Friday after school, I was ________________ through ________________ when I suddenly saw a ________________ spaceship landing in the ________________. It looked like a ________________ and it made a noise like a ________________. The ________________ looked like a ________________. My emotions were out of control—I felt incredibly ________________. I wanted to ________________, but I could not. The ________________ looked at me and invited me into the spaceship. I agreed and, in spite of my ________________, I entered. There were hundreds of ________________ inside. They gave me a gift of ________________, which made me feel at home. The ________________ invited me to travel to ________________ in the spaceship. I said that I was up for the adventure, so we left. When we got there, I met ________________ and all day the crew and I ________________ and ________________. By the time we reentered the spaceship, I was exhausted, but I could not wait to get home and tell my family.

Name ______________________________ Date ____________________

51. What's in a Name

Novelists and playwrights carefully select the names of their characters. Some names are symbolic, while other names suit the characters' personalities. Imagine how differently people might perceive Willy Loman's character in Arthur Miller's play *Death of a Salesman* if, instead of Willy Loman, he had been named William Pensfield Arlington III.

Create names for the following characters that suit their role or personality.

1. An Oscar-winning actress

____

2. A reporter for a sleazy tabloid newspaper

____

3. A coffee shop employee from a Southern town

____

4. A Wall Street investment banker

____

5. A professional boxer

____

6. A wheat farmer from South Dakota

____

7. A homeless beggar from a large city

____

8. A beauty pageant winner

____

9. A scientist

____

Name ______________________________ Date ______________

52. Creating a Character

Before writing a story, a novel, or a play, you should have an idea about what your characters, especially your main characters, will be like. Picture in your mind what they look like, act like, and think like. Know what motivates them, frightens them, and influences them. Use this worksheet before you write a story. Answer the questions about a character on whom you plan to base a story.

1. Is this character male or female? ______________________________
2. How old is this character? ______________________________
3. What is the character's name? ______________________________
4. What does the character look like? ______________________________

   ____
5. Where does the character live? ______________________________
6. What are the character's favorite hobbies, sports, or interests? ______________________________

   ____
7. What does this character do for a living? ______________________________
8. Describe the character's personality. ______________________________

   ____
9. What conflict is this character involved in? ______________________________

   ____
10. What caused the conflict? ______________________________
11. What other character is also involved in this conflict? ______________________________
12. How does this character resolve the conflict? ______________________________

    ____
13. What additional features about this character are important? ______________________________

    ____

Name ______________________________ Date ____________________

53. The Interview

Imagine that you are a famous Hollywood entertainer. You are being interviewed by *People* magazine. An editor has sent you the questions below and would like you to e-mail your answers. Answer each question as you imagine you would if you were a star.

1. What do you like the most about acting and being a celebrity?

2. How did you get your first big break in the industry?

3. What other actors or people inspired you?

4. What is the negative side of being a celebrity?

5. As a celebrity, how do you help others who are not so fortunate as you?

6. What is the moment you are proudest of as an actor?

7. What words of advice would you share with young people who are trying to get into the business?

8. What would you do if you weren't an actor?

Name ________________________________ Date ____________________

54. And Then You Said . . .

When you hear someone talking on the phone, do you ever wonder what the person on the other end is saying? Here is part of a conversation that was overheard. Your job is to write what the other person in the dialogue is saying.

Person A: Did you see that?

Person B: ____

Person A: What was it exactly? I barely saw it.

Person B: ____

____

Person A: WOW! I can't believe that could happen in our neighborhood.

Person B: ____

____

Person A: Well, if you think that's not really strange, then what is the strangest thing you have ever seen?

Person B: ____

____

Person A: Okay, that's bizarre. I'm hungry. What do you feel like eating?

Person B: ____

____

Person A: You actually eat that? I've never heard of anyone eating that. Let me see you eat it because that will be the strangest thing I have ever seen.

Person B: ____

____

Person A: Since when did you become shy?

Person B: ____

____

Name ______________________ Date ______________

55. Opposites Converse

Imagine listening to a conversation between Beethoven and Shania Twain. It might go like this:

> SHANIA TWAIN: So are you a country man or a rock 'n roll man, Beethoven?
>
> BEETHOVEN: I think I prefer living in the country rather than an urban center. But I've never lived near a rock.
>
> SHANIA TWAIN: No. I mean in music. Like what makes you want to dance?

Pick a character from List A who will have a conversation with a character from List B. Then write the dialogue between these two characters. Make sure each character talks the way he/she would in real life.

LIST A	LIST B
Amadeus Mozart	John Lennon
William Shakespeare	Stephen Spielberg
Abraham Lincoln	Oprah Winfrey
Mark Twain	Shaquille O'Neal
Queen Victoria	Meg Ryan

Name ______________________________ Date ____________________

56. Agony Ann Letters

Read the following letters to "Agony Ann." Pretend you are Agony Ann and respond to the letters on another sheet of paper.

Dear Agony Ann,

I am a 15-year-old high school student and my boyfriend is 17. We are totally in love and want to spend the rest of our lives together. My mother thinks we are crazy and are too young to get married. What do you think I should do? Is 15 too young for marriage?

From,

Lovesick in Los Angeles

Dear Agony Ann,

I hate school! In fact I totally hate it. I've never been good at it and I think all the teachers hate me. I want to quit and work for a while. Maybe if I figure out some use for school, then I'll come back. What do you think, Ann? I want some advice.

From,

School sick in Saranac Lake

Dear Agony Ann,

My biggest problem is that I want to be a football player, but the coach won't let me try out for the team. I've always wanted to play football and I practice in my backyard with my dad all the time. The coach says girls can't play football and so the only reason he won't take me seriously is because I'm a female. What should I do?

From,

Wanting to play in Wyoming

Name ______________________________ Date ____________________

57. Word Adding

Write a creative paragraph using as many of the 20 words listed below as possible. Your paragraph must make sense. It may be on any topic you like. (Use the back of this sheet if you need more space.)

HAM	SHOPPING MALL	MITTENS	TRAIN
MARS	TENNIS BALL	MUG	ROCK
FLOWER	ROLLER COASTER	PICNIC	WHALE
CANDLE	STOP SIGN	VALENTINE	DINOSAUR
ARENA	LAB COAT	TELEVISION	OVEN

58. EXTEND-A-STORY

TEACHER INSTRUCTIONS: This is a unique way of writing a story. The students begin this activity by taking out a blank piece of paper and writing their names at the top. Then they begin writing a story. They can write about anything as long as it isn't rude or insulting. (You might want to use the "starters" sheet if students have trouble getting started.)

When you say "start," they begin writing for two minutes. After about two minutes, say "stop" and the students must stop writing and pass the piece of paper to the person behind them. (The person at the end of the row must pass his/her paper to the front.) When you say "start," each person reads what has been written and then adds to the story until you tell the class to stop. This procedure can be repeated for as long as you like.

When the activity is finished, the students return the story to the person whose name is at the top of the paper. The individual will probably have a few chuckles reading the final product.

Incidentally, keep in mind that as the activity progresses, you need to give the students enough time to read the story before they start writing again.

Here is an example of an EXTEND-A-STORY:

One day when it was quite hot outside, Megan decided to go for a swim in her cool, blue pool. When she got to the edge of the diving board, she froze in terror over what was floating along the pool's surface. It looked like a huge monster with long arms reaching out through the water. Little did she know that it was not a monster at all, but the pool vacuum cleaner. But Megan was so scared that she was convinced it was a monster. She screamed for help. A neighbor **heard her cry and called 911. The neighbor also called 16 of her near and dear friends. Before Megan could say "Jackie Robinson," there were hundreds of people in her backyard. By this time** Megan realized that it was not a monster. She did not want to look foolish, so she quickly convinced her brother to dress in a Halloween costume. He did and he ran around the backyard looking scary. Believe it or not, everyone fell for it. The police left scared. The firefighters left scared. Even the neighbor and her gossipy friends left scared. In fact people WERE SO CONVINCED THAT THEY TOLD THE STORY TO THE NATIONAL ENQUIRER. THE PAPER DID A FRONT PAGE STORY ON MEGAN'S POOL MONSTER AND MADE MEGAN FAMOUS. NOW SHE HAS LOTS OF MONEY AND HAS NEVER SEEN A MONSTER IN HER POOL SINCE.

58A. Extend-a-Story Starters

Occasionally students have difficulty getting their extend-a-story started. Below is a list of story starters to assist the student who has writer's block.

1. He opened the closet door in his grandmother's house and could not believe what he saw.
2. The weirdest vacation she had ever taken was to a desolate place known to the locals as . . .
3. Karen and Pete built a time machine in the garage. It was finally complete and they were ready to go on their first journey back in time to . . .
4. Marni had never won anything in her life, but this time was different. She had just won a . . .
5. People never understood why the Reid family kept a ____________ in their backyard. But they said they had their reasons.
6. A purple elephant fell from the sky and landed on . . .
7. On a calm evening in a place where nothing out of the ordinary happens, Claudette's car came to life and told her . . .
8. On a trip to Europe, something happened to me on the plane.
9. The genie told Ajay that he would become a famous person one day if he . . .
10. It was the game of a lifetime and the team should have won except . . .
11. When Dzuy was five years of age, the funniest thing happened to him in kindergarten. It all began when he . . .
12. Jason fell asleep in class and when he woke up a roller coaster was in the classroom. Then he noticed a . . .
13. Before he knew it he was flying to . . .
14. She wasn't sure why she volunteered to go to . . .
15. Strange things happen in the kitchen at 2 o'clock in the morning.

Name ______________________________ Date ________________

59. Write the Beginning

Here is the ending of a story. Create the beginning and middle of this story so that the ending makes sense. (Use the back of this sheet if you need more space.)

Now Chris understood why Jamie showered her/him with gifts and attention. Now she/he understood why Jamie cared so much about her/him. It was too bad though, that like so many things in life, Chris did not know the secret earlier because it would have made such a difference in the final words she/he spoke to her/his cousin.

____
____
____
____
____
____
____
____
____
____
____
____
____
____
____
____
____
____
____
____

Name ______________________________ Date ____________________

60. Finish the Story

The following is the beginning of a short story. Read what has already been written and then complete the story. (Use the back of this sheet if you need more space.)

And the tests were in. And the results were positive. And they were silent: the doctor and him. There was nothing left to say.

He staggered out of the doctor's office and raced down the steps. As he descended, he counted—there were 27 steps.

The parking lot was packed. He watched as a 20-year-old Volkswagen Bug backed into a spanking new BMW. The driver of the Bug inspected the car that his had just met, then drove off quickly. In the BMW's fender was a large dent. He found his car and checked the fender—there was no dent. He got in the car, slammed the door, and revved the engine.

Name ______________________________ Date ________________

61. Knowing Your Audience

Writers should always have a specific audience in mind. Your writing will be more effective by knowing your audience. For example, you would not call the "wicked witch" a "nefarious witch" if you were writing a story for kindergarten students. Here are some things you should know about your audience:

gender	where they live	interests and hobbies
age range	education level	any other important facts

This exercise will help you focus on your audience. *Instructions:* You have been asked to write the following articles. Based on the title and information given, what do you know about the people who will probably read each article?

1. A Study of Jewish Heritage: A recent study done by a Harvard student reveals that Jewish female college students know more about their heritage than Jewish male college students.

   Facts about the audience: ______________________________

   ____

   ____

2. Hockey Players: Are They Better Athletes than Football Players?

   Facts about the audience: ______________________________

   ____

   ____

3. Girl Power: Large companies try to encourage teenage girls to study math and science by offering them big scholarships for college.

   Facts about the audience: ______________________________

   ____

   ____

4. A Home Away from Home: Tips for seniors on what to look for when picking a nursing home.

   Facts about the audience: ______________________________

   ____

   ____

62. A Warm Fuzzy

Teacher Instructions: This writing exercise is an opportunity to give each student a warm fuzzy. Have each student put his/her name at the top of a blank sheet of paper. Then the student should pass the paper to the person next to him/her while that person receives a paper from someone else. The objective of the exercise is for every person to write a positive comment about each individual on the sheet of paper with that individual's name at the top. At the end of the exercise all the students will have a sheet of paper full of positive comments from their peers. The only rule is that no one can write anything negative!

Here is a sample of a warm fuzzy:

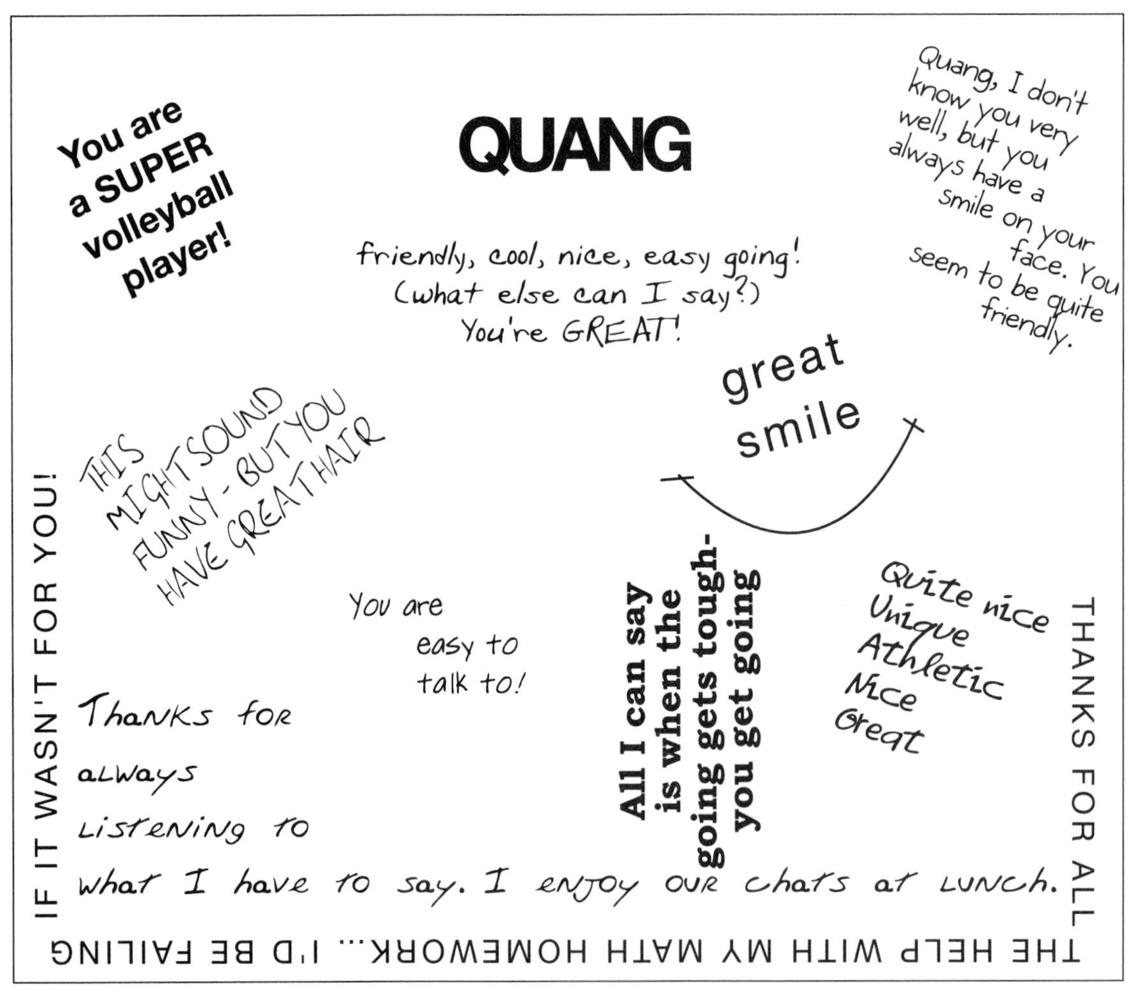

Name ______________________________ Date ____________________

63. Where Will I Be Ten Years From Today?

Describe what you will be doing 10 years from now. If you are stuck for ideas, answer the following questions:

1. Will I be married? To whom?
2. Will I have any children? How many?
3. Will I be at school or working? Where?
4. Where do I think I will have traveled?
5. What types of things will I own? (a car, house, boat, etc.)
6. Where will I be living?
7. What will be my biggest accomplishment at that point?

When you get home today, seal this sheet in an envelope and write the date 10 years from today on the front. Tuck this envelope away. When you open it 10 years from now, you should either have a good chuckle or be shocked at how perceptive your predictions were.

IN 10 YEARS FROM NOW, I WILL . . .

Name ________________________________ Date ____________________

64. Advertising Slogans

Advertising is a billion-dollar industry and advertisers are paid a great deal of money to come up with simple but catchy advertising slogans. Think of Nike's slogan "Just Do It." Three simple words, but the slogan is catchy and has become a popular phrase. Imagine that you are a copywriter for a large advertising agency in New York. You have been hired to come up with a catchy, creative slogan for each product or service listed below. *Helpful hints:* Avoid using unnecessary words in your slogan. Use active verbs instead of passive verbs.

1. **Product:** BIC pens
   Your slogan: ________________________________

2. **Product:** Ford cars
   Your slogan: ________________________________

3. **Product:** A grocery delivery service for seniors
   Your slogan: ________________________________

4. **Product:** McDonald's Big Mac
   Your slogan: ________________________________

5. **Product:** Tours of the White House
   Your slogan: ________________________________

6. **Product:** AT&T Long Distance
   Your slogan: ________________________________

7. **Product:** IBM Computers
   Your slogan: ________________________________

8. **Product:** Revlon Lipstick
   Your slogan: ________________________________

65. Writing a Newspaper Story

Newspaper articles are written in a factual tone. They always answer the questions *Who? What? When? Where?* and *How?* After reading a few newspaper articles, write one by using the following facts from a police report.

—Date: last Wednesday

—Man wearing a Mickey Mouse mask and a construction hat entered a bank.

—The bank is a branch of First National.

—The bank is located on Main Street.

—The man had a gun.

—He took hundreds of dollars in cash.

—He left the bank in under five minutes.

—The theft happened at 2:27 P.M.

—No one was hurt.

—The man did not realize that his name was on the front of his construction hat.

—Cathy Arnold, a teller, called the police.

—Cathy Arnold was the teller the man robbed.

—The police found the robber at his home counting the money.

—The robber's name is Jefferson Jackson III.

—The robber is a millionaire.

—The robber owns a construction company.

—The robber will appear in court next week.

—The robber plans to plead guilty.

Name ____________________________________ Date ____________________

66. Writing a Good Thesis Statement

A thesis statement is usually one sentence (although occasionally it is more than one) that indicates the point of view of the essay, the arguments under discussion, and the order in which they will be discussed.

Here is a good thesis statement:

I like gymnastics because I have fun doing it, I find it a challenge, and I am good at it.

It is clear that the point of view of the essay concerns the reasons the author likes gymnastics. The three proofs that the author plans to use to support the claim that she/he likes gymnastics are:

1. She/he has fun doing it.
2. She/he finds it a challenge.
3. She/he is good at it.

In the essay, this author will write about the first point in the first body paragraph, the second in the second body paragraph, and the third in the third body paragraph.

Here are three poorly written thesis statements. Discuss why they are weak statements and then rewrite them to make them better.

1. In this essay I will discuss why smoking is bad for you.

 ____

 ____

2. My friends mean a lot to me.

 ____

 ____

3. The subject of this paper is that the United States is one of the most patriotic countries in the world.

 ____

 ____

4. There are lots of characteristics that make a person a good friend.

 ____

 ____

Section 3

READING

"Reading furnishes our mind only with materials of knowledge; it is thinking [that] makes what we read ours."

John Locke

Name ______________________________ Date ____________________

67. ESSAY INTRODUCTIONS

One of these introductions is better written and hence easier to read than the other. Read the two introductions and, in the space provided, determine which one is better and why.

Introduction A

Ever since I was a child, I have heard people say that smoking is bad for me. Although I am a nonsmoker, I have come to believe that smoking has some benefits. In fact, it may sound odd to hear me say this, but I believe smoking is actually good for society. For example, the taxes from cigarettes can be quite useful and can generate money for badly needed social programs. Furthermore, going out to smoke a cigarette offers many people a social network that they may not have had without their smoke breaks. Finally, smokers and smoking give people who need to be negative something relatively nonthreatening to complain about. For people who need money for social programs, for people who need a social network, and for people who need something to complain about, smoking provides many benefits.

Introduction B

It is bad to smoke. Everyone knows that smoking is negative. I have always known that it is bad. However, some people think that smoking is positive. I, myself, think it is positive for three reasons. The first reason is that cigarette taxes provide money. This money can help finance social programs. Social programs are seriously underfunded in this country. My aunt, who lost her husband three years ago, gets money from social programs. She is also a heavy smoker. The number two reason is that smoking provides friends. The number three reason is that smokers provide something for complainers to complain about. These three reasons are why I think smoking is good, and I will discuss these reasons in my essay.

Comments:

____

____

____

____

____

____

____

____

____

____

Name ________________________________ Date ____________________

68. Answering the Famous Five

Every news story must answer the famous five questions: *Who? What? When? Where?* and *How?* Many news stories do not answer the question *Why* because the writer may not necessarily know the answer. For instance, a journalist may not know why a robber robbed a bank or why a fire got started. However, the other questions must still be answered. Read the news story below and find the answers to the famous five questions.

Last night, six bulls who are part of the Bull Riding competition were stolen from the bull pens at the Nebraska Big Rodeo.

The missing bulls were discovered by Patty Carr, one of the event coordinators, at 5:30 A.M. when she went to check on the animals.

Carr discovered tire tracks near the pen and the smashed gate. She called the police. The police are currently investigating the situation.

The rodeo Bull Riding competition will continue as scheduled.

WHO? ____

____

WHAT? ____

____

WHEN? ____

____

WHERE? ____

____

HOW? ____

____

____

____

Name ______________________________ Date ____________________

69. Subjective or Objective

News stories can be subjective or objective. *Subjective* means the thoughts expressed are someone's personal opinions and not necessarily based on facts, while *objective* means free from personal feelings and solidly based on facts. Sometimes a news story is a combination of subjective and objective sentences.

Read the news story below. Decide whether each sentence is subjective or objective and be prepared to explain what makes it so.

FIRE AT HOLY CROSS CHURCH

The family of Stuart Kennedy can't believe what happened to the child they all thought was perfect. Around midnight last night Kennedy set the Holy Cross Church on fire.

Neither the police nor family members can explain why this polite, kind, responsible child burned down the church.

"It really isn't in Stuart's nature to start fires or partake in rebellious acts," said the boy's uncle, Henry Kennedy.

Holy Cross Church has been the home church for the Kennedy family for four generations.

Some people at his school wonder if Kennedy's aggression stems from his parents' divorce and his father's upcoming nuptial, which was to take place at Holy Cross.

Damage from the fire is estimated at $100,000.

Kennedy is currently being held at a juvenile detention center while he undergoes psychiatric examination.

Sentence 1: ____________________

Sentence 2: ____________________

Sentence 3: ____________________

Sentence 4: ____________________

Sentence 5: ____________________

Sentence 6: ____________________

Sentence 7: ____________________

Sentence 8: ____________________

Name ______________________________________ Date ____________________

70. Putting the News Story in Order

A news story is written like an inverted pyramid.

- The most important information and answers to the questions *Who? What? When? Where?* and *How?* usually appear at the top of the article.
- The brief, irrelevant facts appear at the end of the article.
- Another standard guideline: The first time a person's name is mentioned, the first and last names are given. Afterwards, the person is usually referred to by his/her last name only.

Using the above information, put the following newspaper article together by numbering each paragraph in order.

____ When fired as a taxi driver from Al's Taxi, Davis held taxi company owner, Al Pacheco, hostage for 24 hours. After a year in prison, Davis was released and offered the position at St. Mary's Church.

____ This is the second time in two years that Davis has been fired, and in both cases he did something drastic for revenge.

____ On Wednesday afternoon a fire, which started at St. Mary's Church, raced along Albany Road and destroyed three homes as well as the church. Fortunately, no one was injured. Joe Davis, the church custodian, has been charged with starting the blaze.

____ Davis is in custody and will appear in court on Monday.—AP

____ **FIRE ON ALBANY STREET**

____ Police suspect Davis may have had help in setting the fire. They request that any witnesses should please contact them.

____ It is believed that Davis, who was fired on Tuesday from the church, set the fire in the church basement at noon. He intended to destroy the church as revenge for the firing.

71. Todd's Wig

Read the following short story. When you are finished, answer the questions on sheet 71A. Do not examine the story again once you have started answering the questions.

Flipping through the family photo album, I came to a picture of my brother Todd, wearing his wig, and could not stop laughing. It has been 12 years since that picture was taken, but it seemed just like yesterday when Todd appeared at my apartment door with a brown paper bag in hand.

"Deerhurst is going to fire me," he said.

"What did you do this time?" I asked. Todd was always getting into scrapes over his job as a room service waiter at the exclusive resort, Deerhurst.

"I didn't do anything. It's my hair. Either I cut it or they fire me."

Ever since Todd turned 16 and decided he wanted to join a rock band, he'd been growing his hair. His hair now reached halfway down his back. "If I want to be a rock star someday, then I need my long hair. It's taken me too long growing it to cut it off now."

"But what about your job?" I asked.

"I think I've got a solution, but I need your help." With that Todd opened the bag and pulled out a woman's short hair wig. It was the kind of wig I could see my 80-year-old grandmother wearing, but not my 20-year-old brother.

"I tried to get a man's wig, but they're too small. They only cover the bald spots and there was no room for my hair."

"How can I help you?"

"You're a hairdresser. I want you to trim it and style it a bit so it doesn't look so old ladyish."

So for the first time in my hairdressing career, I styled a woman's wig for a man. The next day at Deerhurst, Todd wore the wig and kept his job. Even though years have passed since Todd worked at Deerhurst, people still talk about him and his wig.

Name ______________________________ Date ____________________

71A. Questions for "Todd's Wig"

Circle the appropriate answer after reading the story "Todd's Wig."

Remembering the Story

1. What is the occupation of the narrator?
   a. police officer
   b. room service waiter
   c. hairdresser
   d. singing teacher

2. Where did Todd work?
   a. a restaurant
   b. a concert hall
   c. a resort
   d. a hotel

3. Why did Todd wear a wig?
   a. Because he had cancer and lost his hair.
   b. He was embarrassed about being bald.
   c. He thought it looked cool.
   d. He did not want to cut his hair.

4. How long had it been since the picture of Todd in his wig was taken?
   a. 4 years
   b. 12 years
   c. 8 years
   d. 16 years

5. The narrator thought the wig looked like something a _______ would wear.
   a. grandmother
   b. fashion model
   c. bald man
   d. hippie

Understanding the Story

6. What word would best describe Todd?
   a. creative
   b. rude
   c. hyper
   d. wild

7. What is the main idea of the story?
   a. People must conform to society.
   b. People can still conform to society and express their individuality at the same time.
   c. Where there is a will, there is a way, but only if you break some rules.
   d. Not conforming can get you fired.

8. How would you describe the sister's relationship with Todd?
   a. hostile
   b. supportive
   c. jealous
   d. comical

Name ______________________________ Date ____________________

72. Dear Mr. Twain

Read the fictional letter and answer the questions that follow. Circle the correct answers.

Dec. 13, 1876

Dear Mr. Twain,

My sister gave me a copy of your latest novel, The Adventures of Tom Sawyer, for my birthday a few days ago, and the first page was so gripping that I could not put it down until I finished it. I'm writing this letter to express my enthusiasm and gratitude to you for writing such a delightful tale. You made the South come alive! And as a woman who has never had the pleasure of visiting the South, your vivid description made me feel like I was stomping through familiar territory. Although I enjoy writing poetry in my spare time, I can't imagine the time and energy it takes to produce such a lengthy and fine piece of literature. Also, Tom is such a charming character that I'd like to meet him in real life. Since it is impossible for Tom to jump out from the pages and join me for tea, perhaps I'll have the pleasure of meeting him again in another of your novels.

Thanks again for creating such a wonderful read.

Sincerely yours,

Emily Dickinson

1. In this letter, Emily admits that she writes. What, however, does Mark Twain learn that she has never written?
   a. poetry c. a novel
   b. a short story d. an essay
2. From this letter, Mark Twain can assume that Emily Dickinson has never lived or visited which state?
   a. Maine c. New York
   b. Massachusetts d. Georgia
3. In which month is Emily's birthday?
   a. May c. November
   b. December d. June
4. The tone of the letter can be described as
   a. sarcastic c. colloquial
   b. congratulatory d. optimistic
5. The salutations and closing of the letter indicate that the two writers are ________.
   a. close friends c. old-fashioned and stuffy
   b. unmarried d. not well acquainted

Name ______________________ Date ______________

73. A Letter

Read the letter and answer the questions that follow in the spaces provided.

March 15, 2001

Dear Little One,

You have now spent two months in my belly. I hope it's warm and safe in there. You are not big enough for me to see your presence, but I know you're there. It's late and I'm excited because I had my first appointment today, and the doctor confirmed to me what your father and I have suspected for weeks now.

I can't wait to see your face and your toes and your fingers. I can't wait to touch you and know that you are real. You should be healthy if you are anything like me. I rarely eat junk food and I bike 3 miles four times a week. I've been biting my nails a lot lately because I'm nervous about how I'll be as a mom. I'm as new to this parenting game as you are to the baby game, so we'll grow together.

Goodnight my sweet, young (very young) baby.

I'll see you soon.

Love,

M.

1. Who is "Little One"?

____

2. In what month will the writer of the letter's baby be born?

____

3. What is one of M's nervous habits?

____

4. How many other children does M have?

____

5. How do we know that M must be in good shape?

____

6. What mood was M in when she wrote this letter?

____

Name ______________________________ Date ____________________

74. Picnic Insects

Read the article and answer the questions that follow. Circle the correct answers.

They are famous for pestering us at picnics, but really they bother us just about everywhere. What are they? They're ants: six-legged insects, 1/4 of an inch in length, with two multi-purpose antennae. Unlike most other insects, ants have waists, along with a tough outside skeleton.

They live all over the world in colonies, and each colony has a significant ant known as the queen. The queen's job is to lay eggs. The other ants in the colony have specific roles as well. Some construct the nest; some tend to the young; some gather food; some clean the nest; some defend the nest. Like humans, everybody works in the world of ants.

There are 10,000 different kinds of ants, and they come in a variety of colors. Most ants, however, are either black, brown, or rust in color. Other differences? Some ants can sting. Some ants have eyes, while other ants are blind. One thing, however, they all have in common is if protein-rich, sugar-containing food is left out at a picnic, ants are bound to find it.

1. At one point in this article, ants are compared to _______.
   a. royalty
   b. humans
   c. other insects
   d. food

2. Why are ants unique to other insects?
   a. They live in colonies.
   b. They have a queen.
   c. They have waists.
   d. All of the above.

3. Where is this article least likely to be published?
   a. in a newspaper
   b. in a biology textbook
   c. in an outdoor living magazine
   d. in a sports magazine

4. What does the line "They are famous for pestering us at picnics" tell the reader?
   a. Ants only live in the outdoors.
   b. Ants are attracted to the type of food that humans eat.
   c. Ants enjoy festive occasions.
   d. None of the above.

5. One can assume from this article that the most important job in an ant colony is to _______.
   a. to lay eggs
   b. to tend to the young
   c. to clean the nest
   d. to defend the nest

Name ______________________ Date ______________

75. Reading Ad Copy

Below is a series of copy (that's an advertiser's way of saying *the writing*) for four ads promoting a new type of car. Read the copy and then answer the questions that follow.

Ad 1

When the sun is so hot that you could fry bacon on the sidewalk,
You'll need a cool car to cruise the streets in.
Test drive the brand new Yoshi Convertible.
Put the top down, blare the music, watch people stare,
And let the wind cool you down.
Be the first. Start a trend. Get a Yoshi.

Ad 2

When it's cold, the top goes up.
When it's warm, the top goes down.
When you're alone, you'll look cool.
When you've got the kids, they'll all fit in.
For the family and for you: The New Yoshi Convertible.

Ad 3

Don't let your grandchildren notice your gray hair.
Show them you're still young at heart
(even if they can beat you in a race up the stairs)
by buying a Convertible.
Shed thirty years: Get a Yoshi.

Ad 4

The engine has power: 125 hp to be exact.
There are standard safety features: power lock brakes and dual-side airbags.
It's good on gas: 52 mpg.
And it looks cool.
Buy it for its features and for its looks: The Yoshi Convertible.

Name ______________________ Date ______________

75. Reading Ad Copy *(Cont'd)*

1. Which of the four ads would most likely appeal to teenagers?

   a. Ad 1 b. Ad 2 c. Ad 3 d. Ad 4

2. What is meant by the statement "Don't let your grandchildren notice your gray hair"?

   a. Don't let your grandchildren notice that you are getting older.
   b. Don't let your grandchildren notice that you are uncool.
   c. Don't let your grandchildren notice that you are unaware of the trends.
   d. All of the above.

3. Which ad is most likely to be found in a parenting magazine?

   a. Ad 1 b. Ad 2 c. Ad 3 d. Ad 4

4. Which of the four ads is considering the weather conditions of the Northern States?

   a. Ad 1 b. Ad 2 c. Ad 3 d. Ad 4

5. Why is ad 4 written in a less poetic form than the other three ads?

   a. Because the people to whom this ad is directed do not like poetry.
   b. Because this ad deals with technical aspects of the car and it is difficult to write about these features in a poetic form.
   c. Because the advertising writer probably ran out of poetic ideas.
   d. None of the above.

Name ______________________________ Date ________________

76. E-MAILS

Read the following e-mails and answer the questions below. Use a blank sheet for your answers.

From: Kelly Lamky<klamky@abc.com
To: kklamky@abc.com
Date: Wednesday, January 05, 2002 1:15 PM
Subject: Aunt Florence and another question

Hi Kristy,

Mom just called me at work. Did you know that Aunt Florence is unwell? Apparently they don't expect she'll make it through the night.
I just thought you might want to know. Will you be attending the funeral?

Kelly

From: Kristy Lamky<kklamky@abc.com
To: klamky@abc.com
Date: Wednesday, January 05, 2002 3:21 PM
Subject: RE: Aunt Florence and another question

Hi Kelly,

The twins are down for a nap, so I've just been checking my e-mail. It's hard to believe that their lives began just a month ago, and now Aunt Florence's life is ending. However, at the age of 92 she's had a good life. Depending on when and where the funeral is, I'd like to go. She was so good to us. Remember when she took us to Fenway Park in Boston for baseball games?
I just heard a cry from the bedroom. I better go.

Love,

K

1. What is Kelly's main purpose in e-mailing Kristy?
2. How old are Kristy's twins?
3. What is the relationship between Kelly and Kristy?
4. Where is Kelly e-mailing from?
5. Underline a sentence that indicates that Kelly and Kristy had a close relationship with Aunt Florence.
6. Before e-mail was invented, how could Kelly have communicated this information to Kristy?
7. Why do you think Kelly's e-mail is so short?
8. What reason does Kristy give for keeping her e-mail so short?

Name ______________________________ Date ________________

77. Ingrid's Daytimer

Read this excerpt from Ingrid's daytimer and answer the questions that follow.

Sunday	Monday	Tuesday	Wednesday	Thursday	Friday	Saturday
	1 skate with Dave	2 horseback riding 7-8:30 pm	3	4 acting workshop 8-1	5 go to Chicago (train 7 pm)	6 conference for weekend
7 train leaves for home 4 pm	8 lunch with Sue / see Granny at night	9 horseback riding 7-8:30 pm	10 dinner with Dave	11 dentist apt. 9 am	12 movie & dinner with Dave	13 see play with Karen 8 pm

1. What is a clue from the daytimer that Ingrid does not drive?

____

2. What is an activity that Ingrid probably does every week?

____

3. Ingrid wants to go see a movie with her friend Leslee. Leslee is on holidays from the 1st to the 8th. What is probably the best night for Ingrid to meet Leslee for the movie? Why?

____

4. Which of Ingrid's friends does she see the most socially?

____

5. Describe Ingrid's personality, using the daytimer to explain your answer.

____

____

____

____

____

____

____

____

____

Name ______________________________ Date ____________________

78. Classifieds

Read the classified ads and answer the questions below.

Wedding Dress
Size 10, bought new, used once dry-cleaned, $550 Call 883-1110

Bunk beds, wood (pine), brown $200 o.b.o. 872-1149

Microwave $25, Moffatt Stove $100, Queen bed with Beautyrest mattress $200, Oak dining room suite plus 8 chairs $500, Blue love seat $200, call 817-3352

Kitchen table with four chairs, white, $150 873-2447

Wanted—Sports equipment for kids camp. Will accept financial donations too. 817-4386

Cottage for rent—waterfront, all conveniences, 3 bedrooms. Available Aug. $400/week. Call 817-2691

1990 Toyota Tercel, standard, 2 door, green $2000 o.b.o. Call 675-4540

Love seat sofa bed, navy, excellent condition, $150 o.b.o. Call 898-7812

Free Kittens! 8 weeks old, litter-trained, call 963-2710

GE Clean stove, white, 3 yrs old, $200—818-9273

16' Fiberglass Canoe, excellent condition, 5 yrs old, red. $400 o.b.o. 893-2200

Great deals!
Beautiful mink & fox full length fur coat $650, Rowing machine $40, Men's 10 speed bike $200. Call after 6 pm 893-6721.

1. Describe the people who would probably read these ads.

____

2. Where would ads like this be found?

____

3. How would you describe the way these ads are written?

____

____

4. Why would people advertise such products in this format and not through a television commercial or a large, color magazine ad?

____

____

5. Which ad is selling the most items? (Name all the items from the ad.)

____

____

6. How many ads are selling furniture?

____

Name ______________________________ Date ____________________

79. Subway Mania

Below is a map of a new subway that is planned for a large city. Study the map and then answer the questions.

1. Which station is the farthest north? ______________________________

2. Which stations have animals in part of their names? ______________________________

____

3. If these stations were alphabetized, which would be the last station mentioned?

____

4. If you lived at the southern most part of the city, which station is the one you would most likely go to?

____

5. If you got on at Kennedy Station, how many stations would you travel past before stopping at Kingston Station?

____

6. Which stations connect the Hawkings Line to the College Line?

____

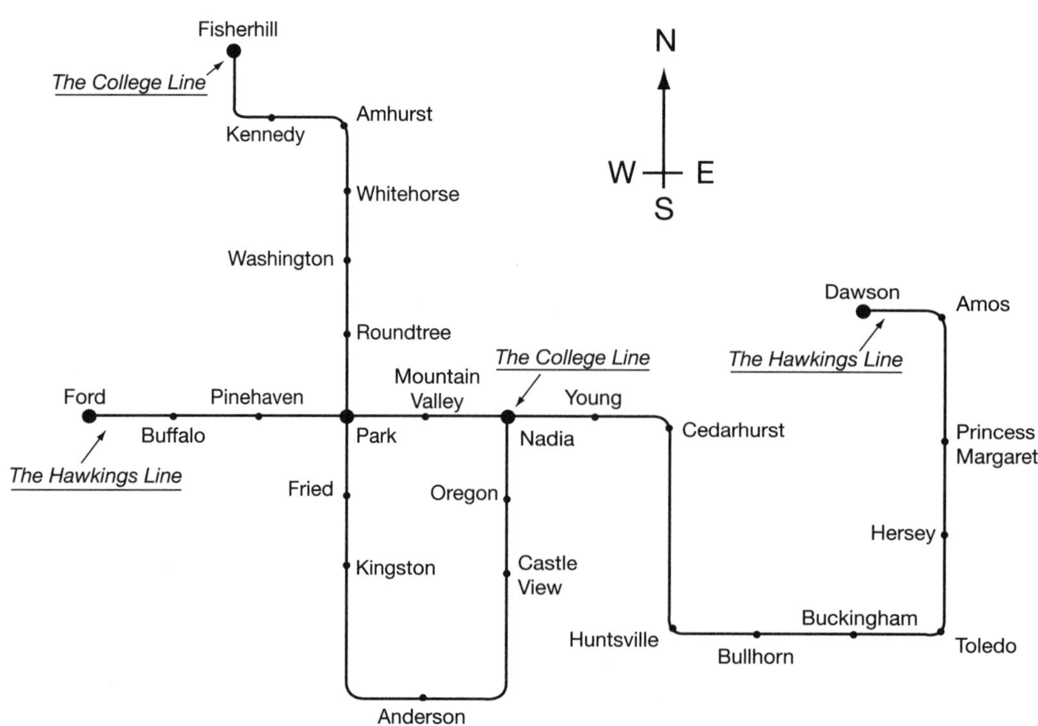

Name ______________________________ Date ____________________

80. The Logic Puzzle

The Dangs, the Dhaliwals, the Kojimos, the O'Connors, the Nguyens, the Salts, the Schwartzes and the Strahms all live on Sussex Drive. From the clues, determine who lives in which house.

1. The O'Connors live in an odd-numbered house while the Schwartzes live in an even-numbered house.
2. The Salts's house number is less than 22.
3. The Dhaliwals live closer to the bus stop than to the mall.
4. The Kojimos and the Strahms have no next-door neighbors at all; while the Schwartzes and the Dangs have neighbors on both sides.
5. On the same side of the street that the Dhaliwals live on, no one else lives whose last name begins with an S.

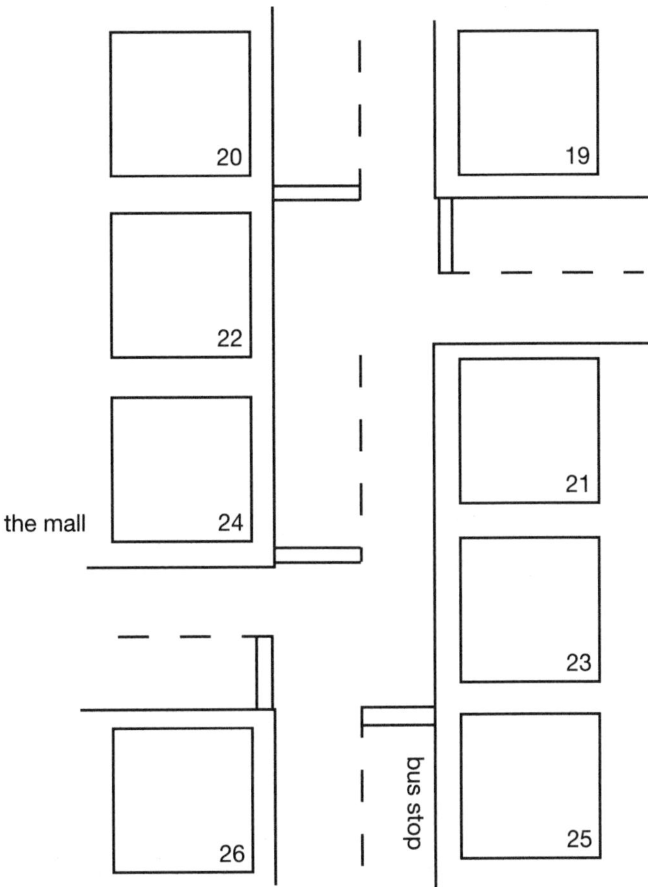

81. Traditional versus Modern

Here are two versions of the original "Cinderella" story—one traditional and one modern. Read the two versions. On another piece of paper write how the messages in the story change from the first to the second version.

The traditional version of Cinderella (adapted from the Grimm brothers' original tale)

Once upon a time lived an unhappy girl named Cinderella. She was unhappy because her stepmother and two stepsisters made her work like a slave. Whenever Cinderella had a spare moment (which wasn't very often), she visited her mother's grave. A little sparrow would watch her as she cried over her misfortune.

One day the prince of a nearby castle announced that he was having a ball in order to find a wife. He would pick his wife from the guests at the ball and so all the females across the country were invited to attend. Cinderella asked her stepmother if she could attend the ball, but her stepmother laughed and replied, "You have too much work to do. And besides, no prince would ever find you attractive enough to marry."

On the day of the ball the stepmother and stepsisters got Cinderella to help them dress for the ball. After they left, Cinderella went to her mother's grave to weep. As she cried, the sparrow flew down from the tree and dressed her in a beautiful gown. Then the sparrow magically created a horse-drawn carriage. Before Cinderella knew what was happening, she was heading for the ball.

At the ball she was definitely the prettiest girl, and the prince spent most of the evening dancing with her. At the end of the night he wanted to propose to Cinderella, but she had disappeared. She was hurrying home before her stepmother returned. On her way home, however, she lost one of her glass slippers.

The next day the prince went all over the land in search of the girl whose foot fit into the glass slipper. He tried it on every girl's foot, but with no luck. Finally, the sparrow flew down on the prince's shoulder and whispered in his ear. The prince went to Cinderella's house and had her try on the shoe. Magically, it fit and she became his princess. They lived happily ever after.

81. Traditional versus Modern *(Cont'd)*

The modern version of Cinderella

Once upon a time lived an unhappy girl named Cinderella. She was unhappy because her stepmother and two stepsisters made her work like a slave. Whenever Cinderella had a spare moment (which wasn't very often), she visited her mother's grave. A little sparrow would watch her as she cried over her misfortune.

One day the prince of a nearby castle announced that he was having a ball in order to find a wife. He would pick his wife from the guests at the ball, and so all the females across the country were invited to attend. Cinderella knew that her stepmother would not let her go to the ball, so she decided to go in secret.

On the day of the ball the stepmother and stepsisters forced Cinderella to help them dress and then they left. Then Cinderella went to her mother's grave and asked the sparrow to help her. The sparrow immediately flew down from the tree and dressed her in a beautiful gown. Then the sparrow magically created a horse-drawn carriage. Before Cinderella knew what was happening, she was heading for the ball.

At the ball she was definitely the prettiest girl there, and the prince spent most of the evening dancing with her. At the end of the night he wanted to propose to Cinderella, but she had disappeared. She was hurrying home before her stepmother returned. On her way home, however, she lost one of her glass slippers.

The next day the prince went all over the land in search of the girl whose foot fit into the glass slipper. He tried it on every girl's foot, but with no luck. Finally, the sparrow flew down on the prince's shoulder and whispered in his ear. The prince went to Cinderella's house and had her try it on. Magically, the shoe fit and he asked her if she would become his bride.

"Eventually I will," she said. "But I need to get to know you better first. Why don't we live together for a few years first. That way I can escape from this miserable stepmother and my horrible stepsisters, and we can decide whether or not we're compatible."

So they signed a prenuptial agreement and lived together for two years before their wedding. And after that they lived happily ever after.

Name ______________________________ Date ____________________

82. Reading Poetry

Read the poem called "In Death" and answer the questions that follow:

In Death

Don't weep for me at the last breath
Because this ending starts a beginning
Of free symphony concerts
        From the chandelier
        Of any concert hall I choose.
My soul will soar to the sky
Using the white fluff as a trampoline.
I'll ballet with the ballerinas
And rebel by bending my knees and flexing my toes.
Perhaps I'll write a play with Shakespeare (if I find the spare time)
Or explore Saturn with Columbus (if his wings are up for it)
        And world tours will be as common as breakfasts
        And ice cream will be cavity free.
Do not weep for me at the last breath.
        For an existence of dreams full of wakenings
        And gravity chains
        Shall dissolve
And at last I'll be able to live.

—S. McTavish

1. What line is repeated at the beginning and the end of the poem? Why do you think this line is repeated?

____

____

2. What is the author's attitude toward death?

____

____

3. Do you agree with the author's view on death? Why or why not?

____

____

4. Underline all the lines in the poem that describe things the author plans to do when she dies.

5. Which line do you like the most? Why?

____

____

Name ______________________________ Date ______________

83. Evaluating Endings

Read the first verse of this two-verse poem, "The Rest of Our Lives." Then read the two endings. One ending is the actual ending of the poem, and the other is not. After reading verse one and the two option endings, answer the questions below.

The Rest of Our Lives

And ninth grade was the beginning of the rest of our lives . . .
Janey was going to be an actress.
Shirley, the Homecoming Queen.
Jillian, medicine. Carol, law.
And Lucy wanted to be something
That I couldn't spell or pronounce
But had loads of money in it.
Myself, I was undecided
With my feet dangling in air
And head lost in the clouds.

Option Ending #1

And Janey won an Oscar (twice).
Shirley became Homecoming Queen.
Jillian, a doctor. Carol, a lawyer.
And Lucy became something
That I still can't spell or pronounce
But there is loads of money in it.
Myself, I finally stopped dreaming,
Got married, had two kids,
And snagged the house of my dreams.

Option Ending #2

And Janey got pregnant at 15.
Shirley married at 21.
Jillian transferred from medicine to Psych.
Good old stable Carol graduated in law.
We all lost touch with Lucy
Although someone said she was somewhere
Richer than Midas, doing something—
I can't remember exactly what.
Myself, I'm still undecided
With my feet dangling in air
And head lost in the clouds.

1. Which ending do you prefer? Why?

____

____

2. If option ending #1 is the ending, what is the overall message of the poem?

____

3. If option ending #2 is the ending, what is the overall message of the poem?

____

4. Which ending do you think is the real one and why?

____

____

Name ______________________________ Date ____________________

84. Dialogue

Dialogue is a conversation between two or more people. Writers almost always use dialogue in their novels or short stories. Plays, naturally, depend heavily on dialogue. Sometimes reading dialogue is hard because it is difficult to follow who is saying what. This exercise will help you improve your reading of dialogue.

Instructions: Below is a dialogue among three people. Read the dialogue, then write it out in the space below as if the dialogue were a play script. This means begin with the speaker's name and then follow with what that speaker says. Do not add any additional information. *Helpful hint:* In this dialogue, every time there is a new paragraph, there is a new speaker.

"I can't believe Aunt Sophie did it."

"Did what?" Jeremy innocently asked his cousin, Jeff.

"Got married."

"Aunt Sophie got married!" Uncle David exclaimed as he joined the conversation.

"When did this happen?" asked a stunned Jeremy.

"On the weekend. Apparently she didn't tell any of us because she thought we'd try to talk her out of it."

"Well, she's right," Uncle David said. "She's 80 years old. Jeff, don't you think she's a little too old to be getting married for the first time?"

"No."

"Yeah, what's wrong with it?" Jeremy continued with his questioning tactics.

"Because she's old enough to have a heart attack with all the excitement," said the uncle.

"Well, at least she'll die happy" was all that the cousin, who broke the news to Jeremy and Uncle David, could say.

____

____

____

____

____

____

____

____

____

____

____

Name ______________________________ Date ____________________

85. What Are They Doing?

Read each passage below and try to determine what the narrator is doing or describing.

1. Dad put the blanket down in the sand. I could hear the crickets crying and frogs croaking in the background. I couldn't see them, of course, because the world was too black. But I wasn't here to see frogs or crickets anyway. We all lay on our backs on the blanket: Mom, Dad, Jeff, and me. Then we looked up in amazement. The night sparkled like diamonds.

   What is the narrator in this passage doing?

   ____

   ____

2. Man oh man! At this moment in the game, I did not need this to happen. I bent down quickly and grabbed one in each hand. I made a loop with the left one. Then wrapped the other one around the loop. Loop through loop and then I squeezed them tight together. That done, I stood up and jumped back into the basketball game.

   What is the narrator doing in this passage?

   ____

   ____

3. Paper first. Then, birch bark (if you have any). Next, tiny twigs. And bigger twigs. The logs will come later. Strike. Strike. AHHHhhh. No wind, please. Phew! It took. The red and orange creatures come to life and dance from the bark of the dead wood. Aaargh! Smoke in my eyes. I better move to the other side.

   What is the narrator doing in this passage?

   ____

   ____

4. She closed her eyes and counted to ten. After screaming "TEN" at the top of her lungs, she began her search. She found Jeremy behind the shrub in Mr. Hamilton's backyard. Lucy was in the tree fort. Now where was Jason? He wasn't in the usual spots: the apple tree or the back shed. There he was. He'd made it back to home base so quietly she never would have caught him.

   What is the narrator describing in this passage?

   ____

   ____

Name ______________________________ Date ______________

86. What Is Being Described?

Read the passage below and answer the question that follows.

> **She felt fear. She felt excitement. Whether she was ready or not, the journey had begun. She saw the tunnel of light and wondered where this journey would take her. Would she be happy there? Would she be safe? So many questions. What would her destination look like? Suddenly she fought back. Suddenly she did not want to go. She kicked and screamed. Was anybody listening? Why did she have to leave? She was warm and safe here. She smiled at the memories and experiences she'd had. But some uncontrollable force was pulling her forward and upward. She helplessly fought back, but it was no use. She took a breath and wailed. Without being able to stop, she was forced towards the light. The journey would soon be over.**

What journey is being described here? Find examples from the passage to support your answer.

Name ______________________________ Date ____________________

87. What Type of Story Is This?

Here is a passage from a classic novel. Read the passage and determine what type of story it is (for example, a romance? A comedy?) Using quotations from the passage, explain why you believe the novel is the genre you have chosen.

The four men went to bed an hour later. They went up together. Rogers, from the dining room where he was setting the table for breakfast, saw them go up. He heard them pause on the landing above. Then the judge's voice spoke. "I need hardly advise you, gentlemen, to lock your doors."

Blore said, "And what's more, put a chair under the handle. There are ways of turning locks from the outside."

Lombard murmured, "My dear Blore, the trouble with you is you know too much."

____

____

____

____

____

____

____

____

____

____

____

____

____

____

____

____

____

____

____

____

Name ______________________________ Date ______________

88. Describe the Shopper

Read each shopping list and, in the space provided, describe the type of shopper who would purchase these items.

Shopping List 1

1) 1 container of wheat germ
2) 1 box of granola cereal
3) 1 bag of Granny Smith apples
4) 1 2-lb. bag of carrots
5) 1 loaf of whole wheat bread
6) 1 quart of skim milk
7) 1 head of lettuce
8) 1 dozen eggs (free range)
9) 1 container of fat-free, plain yogurt
10) 1 package of spaghetti noodles

____

____

____

Shopping List 2

1) 1 dozen buttertarts
2) 1 case of cola
3) 5 frozen dinners
4) 1 package of bacon
5) 1 quart of whole milk
6) 1 bag of salt and vinegar chips
7) 1 frozen pizza
8) 5 steaks
9) 1 bag of potatoes
10) 2 quarts of chocolate ice cream

____

____

Name ______________________________ Date ____________________

89. Directions

Here is a map, followed by some directions. Read the directions and determine where they take you.

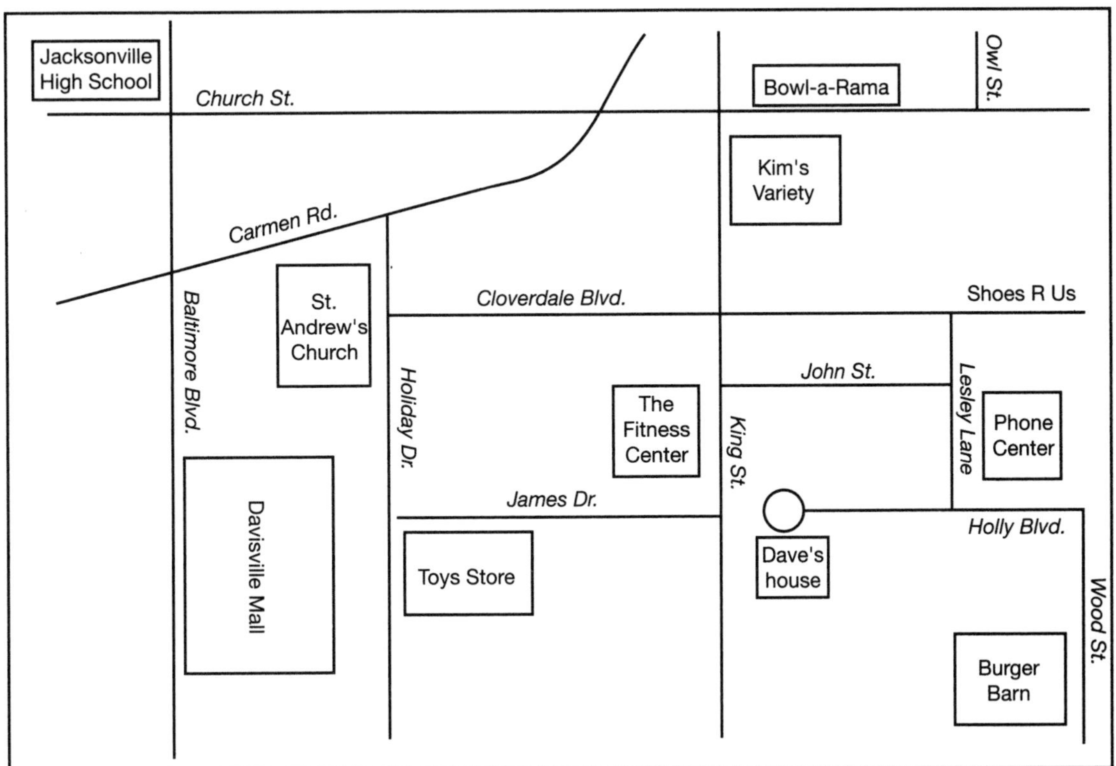

Directions:

Exit from the front doors of Jacksonville High School (these doors face Church Street) and turn left.

Go left through two intersections.

At the third intersection, turn right.

Go through an intersection and then turn left at the next street.

Go to the end of the street and turn right.

At the end of this street, turn right.

Go to the end of the street to the building on your left.

Where are you? ______________________________

Name ______________________________ Date ______________

90. What Are They Saying?

Many great writers have creative ways of expressing simple ideas. For example, rather than simply say, "I was not ready to die, but died anyway," Emily Dickinson expresses this idea in a colorful way when she says:

"Because I could not stop for death—
He kindly stopped for me."

As a reader, it is important that you demonstrate an understanding of what the writer is saying when expressing him/herself creatively. Below each quotation, write in everyday language a sentence or phrase that explains what the quotation actually means to demonstrate you understand the meaning behind the quotation.

1. "If you have built castles in the air, your work need not be lost. That is where they should be. Now put the foundations under them."

—Henry Thoreau

____

____

2. "Nothing is so impenetrable as laughter in a language you do not understand."

—William Golding

____

____

3. "When a dog bites a man, that is not news . . . but if a man bites a dog, that is news."

—John B. Bogart

____

____

4. "Everybody favors free speech in the slack moments when no axes are being ground."

—Heywood Brown

____

____

5. "There's only one real sin, and that is to persuade oneself that the second-best is anything but the second-best."

—Doris Lessing

____

____

6. "The camera makes everyone a tourist in other people's reality."

—Susan Sontag

____

____

Name ______________________________ Date ____________________

91. More Of What They Are Saying

Many great writers have creative ways of expressing simple ideas. For example, rather than simply say, "Tomorrow, life will be better," Lucy Maud Montgomery expresses this idea in a colorful way when she says, "Tomorrow is always fresh with no mistakes in it."

As a reader, it is important that you demonstrate an understanding of what the writer is saying when expressing him/herself creatively. Below each quotation, write in everyday language a sentence or phrase that explains what the quotation actually means to demonstrate you understand the meaning behind the quotation.

1. "To risk is to lose one's foothold for a while. Not to risk is to lose oneself forever."

   —Soren Kierkegaard

   ____

   ____

2. "Thou hast not half that power to do me harm, as I have to be hurt."

   —William Shakespeare *(Othello)*

   ____

   ____

3. "We do survive every moment, after all, except the last one."

   —John Updike

   ____

   ____

4. "Noise proves nothing. Often a hen who has merely laid an egg cackles as if she laid an asteroid."

   —Samuel Clemens

   ____

   ____

5. "A true friend is one soul in two bodies."

   —Aristotle

   ____

   ____

Name ______________________________ Date ________________

92. A One-Minute Mystery

Read the following mystery. Then answer the final question by using the clues in the passage to solve the crime.

Murder or Suicide?

Officer Harold Smucker arrived at the scene of the crime. A suicide note had been scrawled in a messy style that left one with the impression the victim was in quite a state of despair. The victim, Smucker had been told, had been a little depressed lately, and she had seen a psychiatrist for two sessions. In fact, a bill from the psychiatrist lay on the floor near the suicide note. The suicide note was rather ironic because the victim was wealthy and beautiful and seemed to have everything to live for.

Rose petals lay scattered about the room as the naked victim's body hung motionless from the chandelier. A chair, which the victim obviously needed to stand on to reach the noose, lay on its side about 14 feet from the hanging corpse. There were some bruises on the body's legs that Smucker was curious about.

Smucker looked around the room one last time and realized that there was no way this could have been a suicide. It had to be a murder. What made Smucker come to this conclusion?

Section 4

GRAMMAR, PUNCTUATION, AND SENTENCE STRUCTURE

"You can be a little ungrammatical
if you come from the right part of the country."

ROBERT FROST

Name ______________________________ Date ____________________

93. Parts-of-Speech Poem

Here is a list of the eight parts of speech:

NOUN	ADJECTIVE
PRONOUN	PREPOSITION
VERB	CONJUNCTION
ABVERB	INTERJECTION

Fill in the blanks in this poem with the appropriate part of speech.

I know the word *town*

Must always be a ____________________.
And words like *look* and *see*

A ____________________ they'll always be.
But *coach* is a word
That really is absurd
Because, in fact, it could be

A ____________________ or a ____________________, you see.

Blue, wild, new, young, and *old*—

These are ____________________ I've been told.
And when you do not want a noun,

Replace the word with a ____________________.

Because is a ____________________

Under, a ____________________

Wow, an ____________________
I've got "parts of speech" consumption.

And before this poem ends shortly
We've one more to learn rapidly—

An ____________________ is a word like *happily*
And *very* and *far* and *unfortunately.*

Eight parts of speech you now know
So it is time for you to go
And have a welcomed, tiny rest
Before you write the grammar test.

Name ______________________________ Date ____________________

94. Parts of Speech: Analogies

Fill in the blanks with the appropriate words. The first one is done for you.

Nouns

(words that identify a person, place, or thing)

1. MUSTARD : HOTDOG :: COFFEE : ____mug____
2. ALBANY : NEW YORK :: ______________ : CALIFORNIA

Pronouns

(words used to replace nouns)

3. I : WE :: YOU : ______________

Adjectives

(descriptive words)

4. ______________ : GRASS :: YELLOW : SUN

Verbs

(action words)

5. BOOK : READ :: SONG : ______________

Adverbs

(words used to modify or qualify another word)

6. QUICKLY : RACING :: ______________ : TIPTOEING

Prepositions

(words expressing a relationship between a noun or pronoun and another word; example: The man on the platform jumped.)

7. SIT ______________ : CHAIR :: WALK IN : HOUSE

Name ______________________________ Date ____________________

95. Types of Nouns

There are many different types of nouns. Proper nouns represent a specific person, place, or thing and always begin with a capital letter (e.g., Connecticut). A common noun refers to a person, place, or thing in general and does not begin with a capital letter (e.g., tree). Collective nouns are nouns naming a group of things, animals, or people (e.g., flock). Finally, abstract nouns are nouns that cannot be perceived through the five senses (e.g., childhood).

A number of nouns are given in the box below. Put each noun in the chart in one of the four categories that indicates the type of noun it is.

LOVE
Hoover Dam FOOTBALL
FRIEND JURY Justice
Mr. Dhaliwal COMPUTER Gang
North Dakota BEAUTY
TEAM Afterthought
Wednesday class
BOSTON house
friendship committee dictionary

PROPER NOUNS	COMMON NOUNS	COLLECTIVE NOUNS	ABSTRACT NOUNS

Name ______________________________ Date ____________________

96. Collective Nouns

Collective nouns name groups. For example, the word *set* is a collective noun in the phrase "a set of dishes."

In the blanks below, write the appropriate collective noun.

1. **A b___ ___ ___ ___ of cookies**
2. **A c___ ___ ___ ___ of grass**
3. **A stamp c___ ___ ___ ___ ___ ___ ___ ___ ___**
4. **An ant c___ ___ ___ ___ ___**
5. **A d___ ___ ___ of cards**
6. **A f___ ___ ___ ___ of sheep**
7. **A g___ ___ ___ ___ ___ of stars**
8. **A h___ ___ ___ of cattle**
9. **A p___ ___ ___ of gum**
10. **A s___ ___ ___ ___ ___ of fish**

Name ________________________________ Date ____________________

97. Pronoun Fun

Here's an opportunity to learn about a great American while also learning about pronouns. Circle the appropriate answer.

1. Which underlined word is an indefinite pronoun?
   a. Does anyone know that Martin Luther King, Jr. was born on January 15, 1929?
   b. His father's name was also Martin Luther King.
   c. He was known to his family as M.L.

2. Which underlined word is a reflexive pronoun?
   a. Which church was King's home church when he was a child?
   b. It was the Ebenezer Baptist Church in Atlanta, Georgia.
   c. He went back there himself as an adult and became a co-minister with his father.

3. Which underlined word is a demonstrative pronoun?
   a. It was Henry David Thoreau's essay called "Civil Disobedience" that inspired King.
   b. That essay, along with people like Mahatma Gandhi, gave King a strong foundation.
   c. Using this foundation, King challenged the oppression of black people in his country.

4. Which underlined word is a possessive pronoun?
   a. King began his involvement in the civil rights movement after the arrest of Rosa Parks.
   b. Rosa Parks was arrested for not giving up a seat to a person who happened to be white.
   c. As a result of Parks's arrest, King led a successful bus boycott that resulted in the abolishment of segregation laws on buses in Alabama.

5. Which underlined word is a personal pronoun?
   a. Then in 1963 everyone in America learned King's name when he led a mass march in front of the Lincoln Memorial in Washington DC.
   b. Later in 1963, King continued to fight segregation laws when he went to Birmingham.
   c. In 1968, his fight for Civil Rights ended when he was assassinated.

6. Which underlined word is a relative pronoun?
   a. Whoever has not heard of the Civil Rights Movement may still have heard about Martin Luther King.
   b. It is mainly thanks to him that segregation laws no longer exist in our country.
   c. On account of this accomplishment, we remember him on Martin Luther King Day every January 15.

Name ______________________________ Date ________________

98. Pronoun Problems

In each of the following pairs of sentences, one sentence is grammatically correct, while the other sentence has a pronoun problem. Put a check mark in the space next to the sentence if it is correct, and an X in the space next to the sentence if it is incorrect.

________ "Alvaro must choose between you and I," Claudia said angrily.

________ "Alvaro must choose between you and me," Claudia said angrily.

________ When you went on a tour of the White House, we did not see the President.

________ When you went on a tour of the White House, you did not see the President.

________ He and I do not get along anymore.

________ Him and I do not get along anymore.

________ The salesman that came to our door smelled like he had not bathed in a week.

________ The salesman who came to our door smelled like he had not bathed in a week.

________ Everyone is expected to do his duty for the country.

________ Everyone is expected to do their duty for the country.

________ Lucy wants to go to the store with Carmen and I.

________ Lucy wants to go to the store with Carmen and me.

________ We Americans hope to win the most gold medals at the next Olympic games.

________ Us Americans hope to win the most gold medals at the next Olympic games.

Name ______________________________ Date ____________________

99. Verb Tense

Listed below are verb tense definitions and an example of a sentence using the verb tense as defined. Compose your own example of a sentence using the verb tense defined immediately above.

1. PRESENT TENSE: Action that occurs in the immediate present.
   Sample Sentence: She **throws** the football.

   ____

2. PRESENT PROGRESSIVE TENSE: Ongoing action in the present tense.
   Sample Sentence: She **is throwing** the football.

   ____

3. PAST TENSE: Action occurring in the past.
   Sample Sentence: She **threw** the football.

   ____

4. PAST PROGRESSIVE TENSE: Ongoing action in the past.
   Sample Sentence: She **was throwing** the football.

   ____

5. PERFECT TENSE: Action extending from the past to the present.
   Sample Sentence: She **has thrown** the football.

   ____

6. PAST PERFECT TENSE: Action occurring at one point in the past to another point in the past.
   Sample Sentence: She **had thrown** the football.

   ____

7. FUTURE TENSE: Action occurring in the future.
   Sample Sentence: She **will throw** the football.

   ____

8. FUTURE PERFECT TENSE: Action that will have occurred at some point in the future.
   Sample Sentence: She **will have thrown** the football.

   ____

Name ______________________ Date ______________

100. More on Verbs

Determine the tense of the verb that is underlined. Circle the appropriate answer.

1. He is going to my house after work. *The verb tense is:*

   a. Present c. Perfect
   b. Present progressive d. Past

2. He had stopped at the green light. ***Has stopped*** *is which verb tense?*

   a. Perfect c. Past
   b. Past progressive d. Past perfect

3. Jason will go to the bank when he gets paid on Friday. ***Will go*** *is which verb tense?*

   a. Future perfect c. Perfect
   b. Future d. Present

4. Keith was jumping over the fence when Mr. Heffernan caught him. *The verb tense is:*

   a. Past progressive c. Past perfect
   b. Perfect d. Past

5. Carl Lewis runs to the finish line. *The word* ***runs*** *is in which tense?*

   a. Perfect c. Present progressive
   b. Present d. Past progressive

6. Melinda has joined the army. ***Has joined*** *is in which tense?*

   a. Past c. Present progressive
   b. Past perfect d. Perfect

Name ______________________ Date ______________

101. Irregular Verb Forms

Complete the column chart by adding each missing verb and then complete the crossword.

Present	Past	Past Participle
ACROSS		
1. Bleed	_______	Bled
3. Sing	_______	Sung
5. Forbid	_______	Forbidden
6. Grind	Ground	_______
7. Go	_______	Gone
8. Begin	_______	Begun
9. Bring	Brought	_______
11. Do	_______	Done
12. Am	Was	_______
14. Know	Knew	_______
16. Sleep	_______	Slept
17. Tear	Tore	_______

Present	Past	Past Participle
DOWN		
1. _______	Built	Built
2. Drink	_______	Drunk
4. Get	Got	_______
5. Forget	Forgot	_______
8. Beat	_______	Beaten
9. Are (pl.)	Were	_______
10. Hide	Hid	_______
12. Burst	Burst	_______
13. Eat	Ate	_______
15. Write	Wrote	_______
18. Run	Ran	_______

_____________ Date ______________________

JECTIVES, AND VERBS

th the same letter. Then use the three words in a sen-

NOUN ___*dungeon*___
ADJECTIVE ___*dark*___
VERB ___*dance*___

Sentence: *In the* ***dark dungeon,*** *I learned to* ***dance*** *until midnight.*

1. letter **B**

NOUN ________________
ADJECTIVE ________________
VERB ________________

Sentence: ____

____

2. letter **M**

NOUN ________________
ADJECTIVE ________________
VERB ________________

Sentence: ____

____

3. letter **S**

NOUN ________________
ADJECTIVE ________________
VERB ________________

Sentence: ____

____

Name ______________________________ Date ________________

103. Finding Subjects and Verbs

At the beginning of each sentence below is either the word *subject* or *verb.* If the word is *subject,* underline the subject and then write the word in the appropriate space above. (If the word is from sentence #1, then write the word on the blank above #1.) Follow the same procedure if the word is a verb. Once you have finished, the words in the blanks will answer the following riddle:

Why did the man wear a fur coat and a trench coat when he painted the house?

________ ____________ the ________________ on the ____________ ________
(1) (2) (3) (4) (5)

that ____________ ________ ________________ two ________________.
(6) (7) (8) (9)

Helpful hint: The subject and verb is always ONE word in the examples given.

(SUBJECT) 1. He wanted to go to the movies with Clare.

(VERB) 2. Bob read the newspaper every weekday morning.

(SUBJECT) 3. The test instructions confused the students.

(VERB) 4. My friends, who are visiting today, always paint their faces for the football games.

(SUBJECT) 5. The soup can was difficult to open.

(VERB) 6. Wendy and Elizabeth both said hello.

(SUBJECT) 7. On the way to New Orleans, he realized he'd forgotten his suitcase.

(VERB) 8. Arnold needed a friend after his brother's death.

(SUBJECT) 9. There are many coats in the closet.

Name ______________________________ Date ________________

104. Subject–Verb Agreement

In each sentence, one verb does not agree with its subject. Change the verb to the correct form and write the correct word on the line after each sentence. Then put the first letter of the correct verb into the appropriate numbered space above. (For example, for sentence #1, the first letter of the changed verb goes in the space above #1.) This will give you a message about subject–verb agreement.

A ___ ___ ___ ___ ___ ___ ___ ___ SUBJECT NEEDS A
1 2 3 4 5 6 7 8

SINGULAR ___ ___ ___ ___.
9 10 11 12

1. She sing the national anthem every morning. ____________________
2. My drama class are going to the soap opera audition this weekend. ____________________
3. Neither Marie nor David notice your haircut. ____________________
4. The committee give its evaluation soon. ____________________
5. Susan and Sarah understands all the information on the test. ____________________
6. Everyone love my friend Samantha because she is so cute. ____________________
7. My brother, along with his friends, argue that Tiger Woods is the greatest golfer of all time.

   ____
8. The cost of medication, along with doctors' fees, run many senior citizens into debt.

   ____
9. All of my friends votes for Dragana to become the school president. ____________________
10. She is the teacher who always eat in the staff room. ____________________
11. The athletes on the track team runs around the track as part of their warm-up.

    ____
12. My thirty-pound weight gain after the cruise break the scale. ____________________

Name ______________________________ Date ____________________

105. A Sentence or Not a Sentence

Below is a list of song titles. Some of these titles are complete sentences, and some are sentence fragments. If the title is a sentence fragment, put a check mark in the "sentence fragment" column. If the song title is a complete sentence, put a check mark in the "complete sentence" column. Then rewrite the sentence fragments to make them complete sentences.

COMPLETE SENTENCE	SONG TITLES	SENTENCE FRAGMENT
	"Any Man of Mine"	
	"This House Is Not a Home"	
	"Go West"	
	"If I Had a Million Dollars"	
	"I Guess That's Why They Call It the Blues"	
	"I Wish I Felt Nothing"	
	"Hand in My Pocket"	
	"To Use My Imagination"	
	"Raindrops Keep Falling on My Head"	
	"On the Road Again"	
	"Help Me, Rhonda"	
	"A Taste of Honey"	

Name ______________________ Date ______________

106. Book Titles and Sentence Fragments

Here is a list of titles from novels and plays. All of these titles are sentence fragments. Add enough words to each title to make a complete sentence. You may add phrases or clauses to the beginning or the end, but do not separate the words in the title.

1. *To Kill a Mockingbird*

   ____

   ____

2. *A Prayer for Owen Meany*

   ____

   ____

3. *As I Lay Dying*

   ____

   ____

4. *Death of a Salesman*

   ____

   ____

5. *The Catcher in the Rye*

   ____

   ____

6. *The Beast in the Jungle*

   ____

   ____

7. *Looking for Mr. Green*

   ____

   ____

Name ______________________________ Date ________________

107. Running Away with Run-On Sentences

A run-on sentence is a sentence with too much information or inadequate punctuation. In this exercise, put a check mark beside a sentence that is NOT a run-on sentence. If the sentence is a run-on, put an X on the space at the beginning of the sentence and then correct the problem. Then put the first word of the sentence (for the incorrect sentences) in order in the spaces at the top of the page (e.g., the word from the first incorrect sentence goes in the first space on the left and so on).

The words in the spaces will answer the following question:

If a plane crashed on the Canadian and American border, in which country would you choose to bury the survivors?

________________! __________ ________________ __________

________________ ________________!

____1. The snow has stopped; we can go home now because the roads should be clear.

____2. Nowhere will you find such a happy bride, she radiates her happiness her groom must be so lucky to have chosen her as his wife.

____3. Why did she write her essay on *Romeo and Juliet* I would like you to know that she never even finished the play in fact she ended up renting the movie because she had no time to read the play.

____4. In Alaska, winter is more than one season; it's the four seasons combined into a twelve-month marathon.

____5. Would you like to visit Las Vegas someday there is lots to do even if you don't like gambling.

____6. You will find that people who live in New York think it is crazy to live in LA and people who live in LA think it's crazy to live in New York then there are the rest of the Americans who think it is crazy to live in either New York or LA.

____7. Bury compost in the backyard but do not let my neighbor see you do it he doesn't believe in composting.

____8. Survivors are the types of people who make it through difficult times or situations my grandmother became a survivor when she won her battle with cancer.

Name ______________________________ Date ________________

108. Do-It-Yourself Sentences

Create your own sentences by using an adjective + noun + verb + adverb phrase from the chart below. A sample sentence is provided at the bottom of the chart.

ADJECTIVES	NOUNS	VERBS	ADVERB PHRASES
A yellow	priest	found	in a garbage can.
A friendly	skunk	laughs	because his shirt is back to front.
The wild	President	sings	until one o'clock in the morning.
The apologetic	rock star	dances	because the snow has melted.
A sullen	bulldog	races	while the men are wrestling.
A hyper	football fan	marvels	when the pigs escape.
The short	dermatologist	hopes	while she visits the dentist.
The muscular	student	wonders	when his cat plays.
A georgous	boxer	hides	tying his friend's shoelaces together.
The smelly	salesperson	contemplates	because the rain frightens him.

Note: You may wish to alter the form of the verb or add a few words in order for your sentence to make sense.

Sample Sentence: A hyper skunk races when the pigs escape.

Name ______________________________ Date ____________________

109. SUBJECTS, PREDICATES, AND OBJECTS

Here are definitions for subjects, predicates, and objects. Each definition is followed by a sentence. Underline the part of the sentence that demonstrates the definition.

For example, SUBJECTS: Subjects tell what or whom a sentence is about.
Sentence: <u>Judith</u> swims laps at the pool every morning.

1. SIMPLE SUBJECTS: Simple subjects are the specific noun(s) or pronoun(s) that the sentence is about.

   Sentence: This piece of Hawaiian pizza tastes delicious.

2. COMPOUND SUBJECTS: Compound subjects are comprised of more than one noun.

   Sentence: Tom and Randy were bored at the opera.

3. COMPLETE PREDICATE: The complete predicate tells something about the subject.

   Sentence: Judith swims laps at the pool every morning.

4. SIMPLE PREDICATE: The simple predicate is the specific verb that is linked to the subject.

   Sentence: Judith swims laps at the pool every morning.

5. COMPOUND PREDICATE: A compound predicate has more than one verb that relates to the subject.

   Sentence: We walked and talked all night.

6. OBJECT: An object follows a verb and answers *what* or *whom.*

   Sentence: The man drove a new Mercedes.

7. DIRECT OBJECT: The direct object follows the verb and answers the questions *whom* or *what.*

   Sentence: My friend bought tickets to the rock concert.

8. INDIRECT OBJECT: An indirect object is the recipient of the direct object.

   Sentence: My friend bought me tickets to the rock concert.

Name ______________________________ Date ____________________

110. More On Subjects, Predicates, and Objects

Identify the part of each sentence that is underlined.

1. My friend Abby and her sister moved to Kansas City last month.
   a. compound subject
   b. compound predicate
   c. direct object
   d. simple predicate
2. Dennis won concert tickets in a recent radio contest.
   a. compound predicate
   b. simple predicate
   c. indirect object
   d. direct object
3. The class of sixth graders went to the zoo on Tuesday.
   a. simple predicate
   b. simple subject
   c. compound subject
   d. compound predicate
4. Shelley gave Sarah a gift.
   a. simple predicate
   b. compound predicate
   c. indirect object
   d. direct object
5. We ran to meet our father as he walked up the street.
   a. simple subject
   b. simple predicate
   c. direct object
   d. compound subject
6. The students hoped and prayed they passed the final exams.
   a. compound predicate
   b. compound subject
   c. direct object
   d. simple predicate

Name ____________________ Date ____________

111. Phrases, Clauses, and Conjunctions

Below are definitions for phrases, clauses, and conjunctions. Each definition is followed by a sentence. Underline the part of the sentence that demonstrates the definition.

1. PHRASE

   A phrase is a group of two or more words that are linked together, but does not have a subject or predicate.

   Sentence: Of all my friends, I like you best.

2. CLAUSE

   A clause is a group of words linked together that have a subject and a predicate.

   Sentence: Of all my friends, I like you best.

3. INDEPENDENT CLAUSE

   An independent clause can stand alone as a sentence.

   Sentence: We saw the Vietnam Memorial when we visited Washington.

4. DEPENDENT CLAUSE

   A dependent clause (also called a subordinate clause) cannot stand alone as a sentence.

   Sentence: We saw the Vietnam Memorial when we visited Washington.

5. SUBORDINATING CONJUNCTION

   A Subordinating conjunction is the word that introduces a dependent clause.

   Sentence: We saw the Vietnam Memorial when we visited Washington.

6. COORDINATING CONJUNCTION

   A coordinating conjunction joins words and phrases to independent clauses.

   Sentence: Lindsay wants to travel to Maine, but Laura wants to travel to Georgia.

7. PREPOSITIONAL PHRASE

   A prepositional phrase begins with a preposition and any additional adjectives, pronouns, adverbs, etc.

   Sentence: Each of my friends wants to attend the same college.

Name ______________________________ Date ________________

112. More on Phrases, Clauses, and Conjunctions

Identify the part of the sentence that is underlined.

1. <u>If</u> you take a trip to Hawaii, will you buy me a souvenir?
   a. independent clause
   b. coordinating conjunction
   c. subordinating conjunction
   d. prepositional phrase

2. <u>Before Joanne went to the party,</u> she did her homework.
   a. dependent clause
   b. independent clause
   c. coordinating conjunction
   d. prepositional phrase

3. John likes to ski in Vermont, <u>and</u> Marion likes to watch from the warm chalet.
   a. dependent clause
   b. coordinating conjunction
   c. subordinating conjunction
   d. prepositional phrase

4. Justin placed the cards <u>on the table</u>.
   a. independent clause
   b. dependent clause
   c. subordinating conjunction
   d. prepositional phrase

5. <u>I planned to meet Todd and Ian for dinner at eight o'clock</u>, but my bus was late, and I arrived after 8:30.
   a. independent clause
   b. dependent clause
   c. prepositional phrase
   d. coordinating conjunction

Name ______________________________ Date ____________________

113. Types of Sentences

There are several types of sentences. Some sentences are classified by their clause structure, while other sentences are classified by their purpose. Good writers use a variety of sentence types. For each sentence type listed below, there is a brief explanation followed by an example. In each case, identify the clause or subordinate clause. Then write your own sentence illustrating each sentence type.

1. **Simple Sentences:** A simple sentence contains a main clause and no subordinate clauses.

   Example: *All students should learn to read.*

   Your simple sentence: ______________________________

   ____

   ____

2. **Compound Sentences:** A compound sentence contains two or more main clauses that may be joined by either a semi-colon or a coordinating conjunction *(and, but, or, for, nor, so, yet)* and a comma. Compound sentences do NOT have subordinate clauses.

   Example: *My parents took me to Walt Disney World last year, and they took me to the Grand Canyon the year before.*

   Your compound sentence: ______________________________

   ____

   ____

3. **Complex Sentences:** A complex sentence contains a main clause and one or more subordinate clauses.

   Example: *If you decide to take a trip to New York City, I suggest you go to see the Rangers play.*

   Your complex sentence: ______________________________

   ____

   ____

4. **Compound–Complex Sentence:** This type of sentence consists of two or more main clauses and at least one subordinate clause.

   Example: *Even though the city of New Orleans was prepared, the flood waters still devastated the community and many people lost their homes.*

   Your compound–complex sentence: ______________________________

   ____

   ____

Name ______________________________ Date ________________

114. More About the Types of Sentences

There are several types of sentences. Some sentences are classified by their clause structure, while other sentences are classified by their purpose. Good writers use a variety of sentence types. For each sentence type listed below, there is a brief explanation followed by an example. Then write your own sentence illustrating each sentence type.

1. **Declarative Sentence:** A declarative sentence makes a statement.

   Example: *Roxanne bought a new car.*

   Your declarative sentence: ______________________________

   ____

   ____

2. **Interrogative Sentence:** An interrogative sentence asks a question and ends with a question mark.

   Example: *Did Sarah pass her math test?*

   Your interrogative sentence: ______________________________

   ____

   ____

3. **Imperative Sentence:** An imperative sentence issues a command or makes a request. Often *you* is the understood subject.

   Example: *Please turn down the stereo.*

   Your imperative sentence: ______________________________

   ____

   ____

4. **Exclamatory Sentences:** An exclamatory sentence indicates emotion and excitement and ends with an exclamation point. (Sometimes exclamations are not complete sentences.)

   Example: *Great shot!*

   Your exclamatory sentence: ______________________________

   ____

   ____

Name ________________________________ Date ____________________

115. Parallelism

Items in a series must be in parallel form and also in the same grammatical form. The sentence below is NOT in parallel form.

James likes sailing, running, and to sleep.

In order to be parallel, the sentence should read:

James likes sailing, running, and sleeping.

Rewrite the sentences below and correct the parallel problems.

1. Her car is powerful, fast, and it did not cost much money.

____

____

2. His career as a professional hockey player made him physically perfect, prosperous financially, and completely unhappy.

____

____

____

3. In the winter she wants to ski, but she likes surfing when it is summer.

____

____

____

4. I want to go to the concert, but I am too poor, too busy, and I am very sick.

____

____

____

5. He likes his music loud, his food hot, and having his bed made.

____

____

____

Name ______________________________ Date ____________________

116. Misplaced Modifiers

Modifiers are descriptive words. These modifiers become misplaced if placed in an awkward position in the sentence. Misplaced modifiers confuse the correct meaning of the sentence. Place modifiers as close as possible to what they describe. For example:

Teenagers are more likely to buy designer jeans than grandmothers.

This sentence implies that teenagers would rather buy designer jeans than buy grandmothers! Notice that by rearranging the phrase *than grandmothers,* the meaning of the sentence changes.

Teenagers are more likely than grandmothers to buy designer jeans.

Instructions: Study the pairs of sentences below and determine which one is worded correctly and which one has a misplaced modifier. Put a check mark beside the correct sentence and an X beside the sentence with a misplaced modifier.

____ I read in the paper that Janice had her baby.

____ I read that Janice had her baby in the paper.

____ You should always wear a helmet when you ride a motorcycle.

____ You should always ride a motorcycle wearing a helmet.

____ Marni found it difficult to ride her bike wearing tight jeans.

____ Marni, wearing tight jeans, found it difficult to ride her bike.

____ While driving my car, I noticed a house on fire on Elm Street.

____ I noticed a house on fire on Elm Street driving my car.

____ Carlitos left a soda for his friend on the table.

____ Carlitos left a soda on the table for his friend.

Name ____________________________________ Date ____________________

117. Capitalization

There are several capitalization errors in the sentences below. Your job is to add capital letters in the appropriate spots in order to answer the following riddle:

A non-swimmer is stranded on an island a mile from shore. He has no boat, plane, radio, or building materials on this treeless island. How does he get to shore?

_______ _______ _______________ _______ _______ _______________
(1) (2) (3) (4) (5) (6)

_______________ _______ _______ _______.
(7) (8) (9) (10)

Each blank above represents a word made from the corrected capitals in the corresponding sentences.

1. While i was doing the laundry, tammy called.
2. It is rather ironic that the irish man speaks only spanish.
3. when i go to the Cn tower in Toronto, I plan to go at easter and try to visit my grandmother on redmond Street.
4. On saturday he leaves for orlando.
5. They even have heinz ketchup in egypt.
6. why did admiral leacock go to kamsack, south Carolina?
7. aunt cindy is from richmond, my uncle is from ohio, and my friend sandra is from the south.
8. oh, I can't wait to visit norway.
9. this hindu speaks english.
10. i plan to visit chicago with elsie.

Name ______________________ Date ______________

118. Homophones

A homophone is a word having the same sound as another word but with a different meaning and spelling. For example, *deer* and *dear* are homophones. Often homophones are used incorrectly. Below is a list of sentences with the homophones underlined. If the sentence uses a homophone correctly, then shade the number that appears in the chart. If the homophone is incorrect, then make the appropriate corrections. When you are finished, the shaded area will reveal a homophone.

1	2	3
4	5	6
7	8	9
10	11	12
13	14	15

1. Their car was purchased a year ago.
2. I want to go to the Tigers game too.
3. Did you hear the latest gossip from the *National Enquirer?*
4. I did not no that you read that magazine.
5. Why is Liza surprised that there are many Buffalo Bills fans in Pennsylvania?
6. Their going to ski in Vermont this winter.
7. Would you run too the mall with me?
8. You two are a cute couple.
9. Wear did Ian find that bargain?
10. I recently bought a pare of shoes.
11. If Carrie looks in the mirror too often, she will be considered vain.
12. Weather or not you come with me is your mother's decision.
13. The nurse plans to take his 15-minute break soon.
14. Mrs. Thompson plans to dye her hair red.
15. When we buy our car, we plan to pay cash.

Name ______________________________ Date ________________

119. A Homophone Crossword

Homophones are words that sound the same, but are spelled differently (e.g., *your* and *you're*). Each clue in the crossword is a homophone. Determine its homophone in each case and put it in the appropriate spot in the crossword.

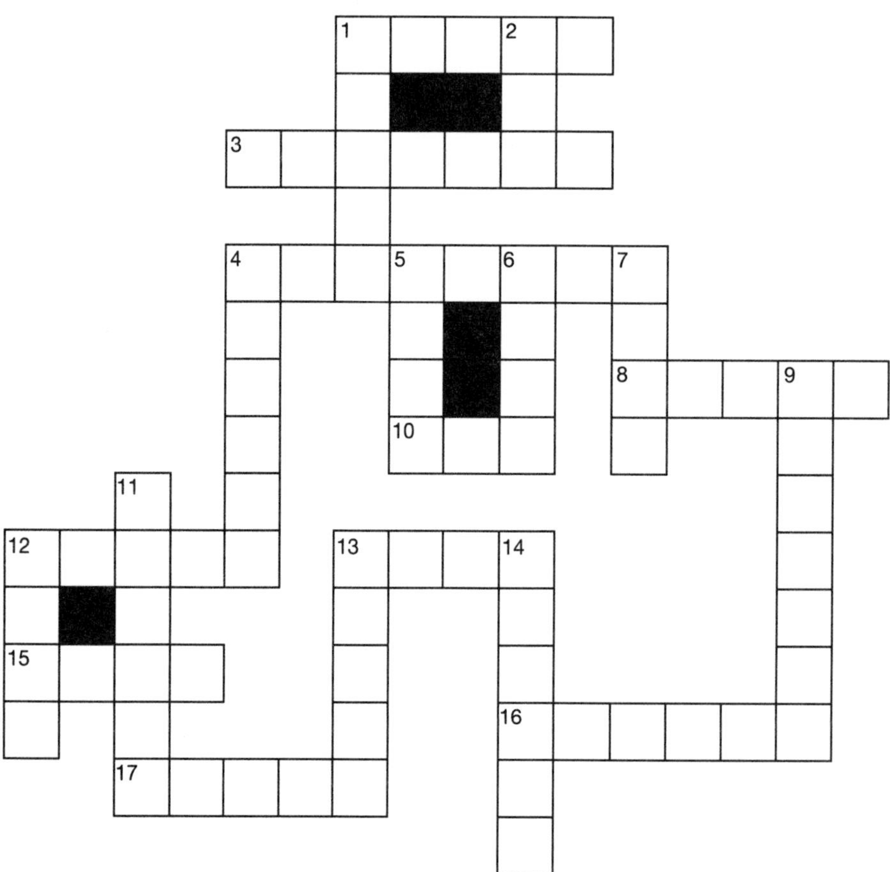

Across

1. STEEL
3. WEATHER
4. PATIENTS
8. RAIN
10. YOU
12. I'LL
13. MAUL
15. KNEAD
16. SIDE
17. THERE

Down

1. CENT
2. AIL
4. PEDAL
5. IDOL
6. NUN
7. URN
9. GUEST
11. ASCENT
12. ANT
13. MINER
14. LESSEN

Name ______________________________ Date ____________________

120. Learning the Rules for Plurals

In PART A is a list of plural rules. In PART B is a list of words in the singular. Change the singular word to plural. Then, in the space on the left of the singular word, write the number of the plural rule that you used.

Part A

1. For most nouns simply add 's' to make the word plural.
2. If the word ends in 's,' 'sh,' 'ch,' 'x,' or 'z,' add 'es' to make it plural.
3. If the word ends in a consonant followed by 'y,' the plural is formed by changing the 'y' to an 'i' and adding 'es.'
4. If the word ends in a vowel followed by a 'y,' the plural is formed by adding 's.'
5. The plurals of most nouns ending in 'f' or 'fe' are formed by adding 's.'
6. Some words that end in 'f' or 'fe' are formed by changing the 'f' to a 'v' and adding 'es.'
7. If the word ends in a consonant followed by an 'o,' form the plural by adding 'es.'
8. If the word ends in a vowel followed by an 'o,' add 's' to make the word plural.
9. For compound words, make the first noun plural.
10. Sometimes the word remains the same in the plural form as in the singular form.

Part B

Example:

7 ZERO ZEROES

____	Deer	______________	____	City	______________
____	Belief	______________	____	Church	______________
____	Door	______________	____	Sister-in-law	______________
____	Video	______________	____	Hero	______________
____	Tomato	______________	____	Moose	______________
____	Success	______________	____	Boy	______________
____	Car	______________	____	Wolf	______________
____	Family	______________	____	Patio	______________
____	Wife	______________	____	Fox	______________

Name ______________________________ Date ____________________

121. Irregular Plurals

Some words have irregular plurals that do not follow conventional rules. Complete the chart by writing the plural and then find the plural in the word search. The words can be found forward, backward, and diagonal.

SINGULAR	PLURAL	SINGULAR	PLURAL
FOOT		WOMAN	
TOOTH		SPECIES	
INDEX		MEDIUM	
AXIS		FOCUS	
BASIS		STIMULUS	
LOUSE		CRISIS	
OX		CRITERION	
CHILD		RADIUS	

F U N Y I J I C O F M W
S E A H Q A O K P L O F
E P E X U J X D E M S G
C W I T Z N E E E T P I
I V S E B C N N S O E L
D U K E H L I C E I C U
N M R T S F R N S I I M
I C G H Q I O L A D E I
D M E D I A R P B A S T
A I R E T I R C S R A S
E T S B N E R D L I H C

Name ______________________________ Date ____________________

122. The Apostrophe: Contraction

A contraction occurs when two words are shortened into one word, and an apostrophe replaces the missing letters. For example, *I will* can be shortened to *I'll.* The apostrophe replaces the letters *w* and *i.*

Part One: Rewrite these words into contractions. (The first one is done for you.)

1. she would ___*she'd*___
2. I am ____________________
3. you will ____________________
4. did not ____________________
5. it is ____________________
6. who has ____________________
7. we are ____________________
8. could not ____________________
9. he is ____________________
10. are not ____________________

Part Two: Rewrite these words with the apostrophes in the correct place. (The first one is done for you.)

1. theyve ___*they've*___
2. isnt ____________________
3. weve ____________________
4. wouldnt ____________________
5. itll ____________________
6. hed ____________________
7. cant ____________________
8. youll ____________________
9. theyre ____________________
10. shes ____________________

Name ______________________________ Date ____________________

123. THE APOSTROPHE: POSSESSION

The apostrophe is used to show ownership or possession. The rules that apply are:

1. When the word is singular and does not end in *s,* add *'s.*
2. When the word is singular and does end in *s,* add *'s* or ' .
3. When the word is plural and does not end in *s,* add *'s.*
4. When the word is plural and does end in *s,* add ' .

Remember, some possessive pronouns (like *their, mine,* and *your)* are already in the possessive form and do not require *'s.*

PART ONE: Put the following words in the possessive form.

1. he ______________________
2. Bryan ______________________
3. Christmas ______________________
4. bosses ______________________
5. women ______________________
6. woman ______________________
7. dogs ______________________
8. Chris ______________________
9. cities ______________________
10. they ______________________

PART TWO: Correct the following sentences by adding apostrophes where necessary.

1. My fathers eldest sisters friend recently was appointed the United States ambassador to China.
2. There are many bulls in the rodeo, but there are not enough bulls pens.
3. In the sixties mens hair was much longer than in the fifties.
4. All of my friends stresses revolve around final exams and the winter blahs.
5. I would rather go to Romans house than to Margarets.

Name ______________________________ Date ________________

124. Quotation Marks

If the sentence uses quotation marks and other punctuation correctly, shade in the areas in the numbered chart. If the sentence does not use quotation marks or other punctuation that relates to quotation marks correctly, then make the appropriate corrections. The shaded area will be a picture of something related to this topic.

1	2	3	4	5	6
7	8	9	10	11	12

1. Anna asked, "When are you going to Sue's house?"
2. In his anger, Carl asked me "to fight him."
3. A & P is my favorite short story in a collection of short stories called "Pigeon Feathers" by John Updike.
4. "Edger Allan Poe" is a famous American poet who wrote a poem called The Raven.
5. My favorite episode from the TV show "Friends" is called The Triplets Arrive.
6. "I can come," Lenny said, "as long as Gillian can come too."
7. "When I write, I shake off all my cares" wrote Anne Frank in her diary.
8. My favorite song has always been "Born in the USA" by Bruce Springsteen.
9. Doug shouted, "Stop yelling This is my day off. I heard you the first time."
10. Otto asked, "Why did Janice leave"?
11. I wrote an essay entitled "The Significance of the Kennedy Family in American Politics" for my history class.
12. "I'm buying my first car next Friday, Mark said."

Name ______________________________ Date ____________________

125. Punctuation Puzzle

Some of the following sentences have punctuation errors. If there is a punctuation error, then make the necessary corrections. If the sentence is correct, shade in the number on the chart that corresponds with the sentence number. When you are finished, the shaded area will reveal a punctuation mark.

1	2	3
4	5	6
7	8	9
10	11	12
13	14	15

1. When are you going to the movie.
2. What can I do if he refuses to see a doctor?
3. Raj Stuart Mary Cam and Sal talked in the cafeteria for the entire period.
4. Connor who owns a store recently filed for bankruptcy.
5. Ian, of course, is always in trouble.
6. Mrs Vijh has lived in Buffalo New York her entire life.
7. She asked her friend when the party started?
8. The accident made Shelly afraid of driving; however, she realized that at some point she must get behind the wheel of a car again.
9. The Canadians built the spaceship's engine, the Americans built the exterior.
10. She wanted to go to Caesar's Palace with you
11. Did she attend the concert too.
12. Usually; we go to the picnic as a family.
13. Are you going.
14. Carlitos, my mother's friend, has been quoted in *The Financial Post.*
15. He said "I realize that the American dollar is in a great position at the moment."

Name ______________________________ Date ____________________

126. Punctuation Dot-to-Dot

Below is a list of punctuation rules. If the rule is correct, connect the corresponding number on the dot-to-dot at the bottom of the page. If the rule is incorrect, change the rule to make it connect. What do you get when you connect the dots?

RULE 1: Use a period at the end of a sentence.

RULE 2: Use a question mark at the end of all indirect questions.

RULE 3: Colons are used to introduce a series.

RULE 4: A semicolon has the same function in a sentence as a comma.

RULE 5: Use a comma at the end of a dependent clause that comes before a main clause.

RULE 6: Quotation marks are used to indicate a direct quotation.

RULE 7: Commas separate two independent clauses that do not have transitional words between them.

RULE 8: A semicolon is used to introduce a dialogue.

RULE 9: A colon is used at the end of the salutation in a business letter (e.g., Dear Sir:).

RULE 10: A semicolon separates two independent clauses that are not connected with linking words.

RULE 11: An exclamation point indicates strong emotion.

RULE 12: A semicolon separates three or more words in a series.

RULE 13: A comma separates three or more words in a series.

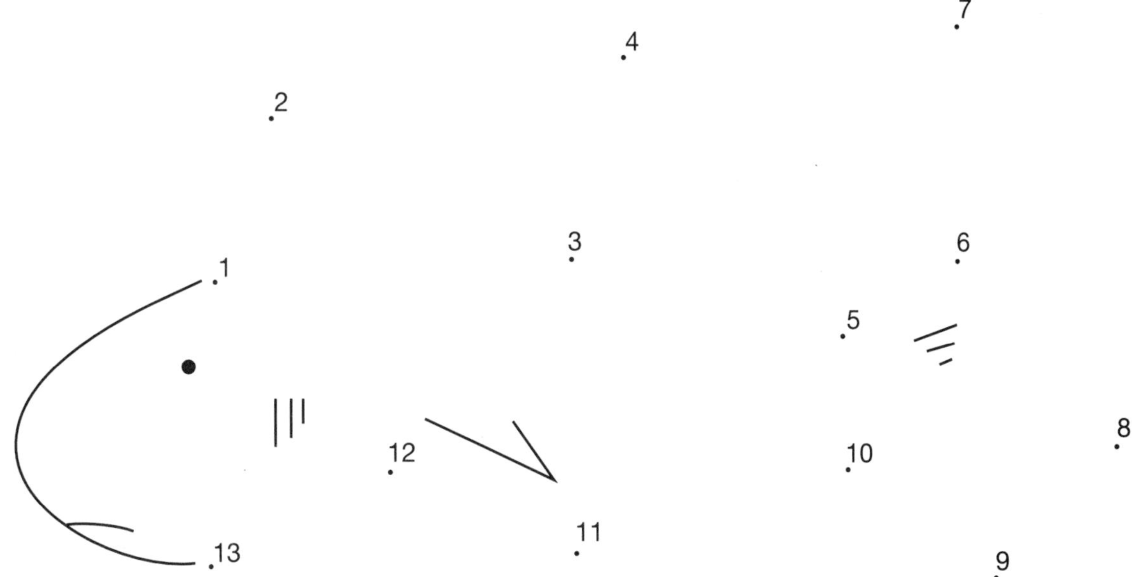

Name ______________________________ Date ____________________

127. Punctuation Multiple-Choice

Read each sentence and circle the multiple-choice option that indicates the correct punctuation.

1. Did you Jessica asked find my sweater

   a. "Did you Jessica asked find my sweater?"

   b. "Did you," Jessica asked, "find my sweater?"

   c. "Did you?" Jessica asked, "find my sweater."

2. A year ago I decided to start studying for the SATS otherwise I thought I might fail

   a. A year ago I decided to start studying for the SATS, otherwise, I thought I might fail.

   b. A year ago, I decided to start studying for the SATS, otherwise, I thought I might fail.

   c. A year ago, I decided to start studying for the SATS; otherwise, I thought I might fail.

3. Elizabeth my friend with red hair wonders if I will go to the beach with her on Saturday July 10

   a. Elizabeth, my friend with red hair, wonders if I will go to the beach with her on Saturday, July 10.

   b. Elizabeth, my friend with red hair, wonders if I will go to the beach with her on Saturday, July 10?

   c. Elizabeth my friend with red hair wonders if I will go to the beach with her on Saturday, July 10.

4. There are a few things however that I want you to get from the variety store milk bread and chips.

   a. There are a few things; however, that I want you to get from the variety store: milk, bread, and chips.

   b. There are a few things, however, that I want you to get from the variety store: milk, bread, and chips.

   c. There are a few things, however, that I want you to get from the variety store, milk, bread, and chips.

Name ______________________________ Date ____________________

128. You're the Editor

Below is a list of common sentence errors with a letter beside each one. The paragraph contains ten of these sentence errors. Each sentence error in the paragraph has been underlined and numbered. At the bottom of the page, write the letter of the sentence error in its corresponding numbered space.

A. Mistake in subject–verb agreement
B. Apostrophe mistake
C. Missing comma after introductory words
D. Sentence fragment
E. Missing capital letter
F. Run-on sentence
G. Irregular verb

I has (1) lived in New York City all my life, and I love it here. Because of the multiculturalism, the activities, and the people. (2) I like it when I go to one friends' house (3) and I hear her family speaking chinese, (4) and at another friend's house I hear Polish. Also (5) there is lots to do in New York. My friends and I like to see the Rangers play in the winter and the Mets play in the summer, however, my parents like to go to the Metropolitan Museum of Art. (6) Finally (7) I like New York because of the people. I have find (8) over the years that New Yorkers are extremely friendly. When people disagree with me. (9) I tell them just to walk up to a New Yorker with a question. New yorkers (10) will always answer with a smile. These are the reasons why I love living in New York.

1. ________ 3. ________ 5. ________ 7. ________ 9. ________

2. ________ 4. ________ 6. ________ 8. ________ 10. ________

Section 5

SPELLING

"My spelling is wobbly. It's good spelling but it wobbles, and the letters get in the wrong places."

A. A. MILNE

Name ______________________________ Date ____________________

129. Able or Ible

Add *able* or *ible* to complete the following words:

1. AGREE ________________
2. CHANGE ________________
3. COMPAT ________________
4. CONVERT ________________
5. DEPEND ________________
6. DESIR ________________
7. ED ________________
8. ENFORCE ________________
9. ELIG ________________
10. HORR ________________
11. IRRESIST ________________
12. IRRIT ________________
13. LEG ________________
14. LIV ________________
15. PLEASUR ________________
16. TERR ________________
17. MEMOR ________________
18. RESPONS ________________

Name ______________________________ Date ______________

130. Adding the Correct Letters

EI/IE

Add either *ei* or *ie* to spell each word correctly.

1. w ________ rd
2. dec ________ ve
3. s ________ ze
4. l ________ sure
5. caff ________ ne
6. n ________ ce
7. w ________ ld
8. c ________ ling
9. rec ________ pt
10. retr ________ ve

ER/OR

Add either *er* or *or* to spell each word correctly.

1. educat________
2. defend________
3. produc________
4. collect________
5. inspect________
6. invent________
7. manag________
8. invad________
9. investigat________
10. visit________

ARY/ERY

Add either *ary* or *ery* to spell each word correctly.

1. cemet ________
2. vocabul ________
3. Janu ________
4. flatt ________
5. bound ________
6. revolution ________
7. element ________
8. bak ________
9. libr ________
10. station ________ (paper)
11. station ________ (not moving)

Name ______________________________ Date ____________________

131. What Is the Missing Vowel?

A vowel is needed in each blank. Place the appropriate vowel in each blank.

1. dis ____ ppear
2. coll ____ ge
3. repet ____ tion
4. bus ____ ness
5. appr ____ ciate
6. prej ____ dice
7. prep ____ ration
8. irrel ____ vant
9. num ____ rous
10. tog ____ ther
11. spe ____ ch
12. summ ____ ry
13. vis ____ ble
14. int ____ rest
15. disc ____ ssion
16. bound ____ ry
17. contr ____ versial
18. sat ____ sfactory
19. priv ____ lege
20. inn ____ cent
21. handk ____ rchief
22. ob ____ dience
23. hist ____ ry
24. amb ____ tion
25. acc ____ rate
26. sal ____ ry
27. sep ____ rate
28. suff ____ cient
29. ski ____ ng
30. explan ____ tion

Name ______________________________ Date ________________

132. Computer Cards and Your Spelling Errors

The following article was put through spellcheck and accepted; however, a number of spelling errors remain. Circle each spelling error and correct it.

Computers have a knew program out now; its called *Make-You're-Own-Cards.* Its a grate idea accept for won problem: spelling. There are lots of words that look like they are spelled correctly but their actually knot. Take, four example, the word *your.* Recently eye received a personalized card that red: "Your the Greatest! Happy Birthday!" Then I received another personalized card that was signed "From you're number one brother." At this point I new they're was a problem. To many people use spellcheck on there computers but fail too proofread they're cards. All the errors that I'm discussing wood knot bee caught buy spellcheck. Its knot that I'm unappreciative of the cards scent too me; its just that I'm concerned that people remember to check there spelling before the card is in it's envelope and in the male. Remember, you, two, can become a spelling master. All you need too due is edit you're material.

Name ______________________________ Date ____________________

133. Problem Words

People often misspell the words in parentheses. Circle the correct word in parentheses in each sentence.

1. Everyone (accept, except) Amos brought a gift to the party.
2. Lung cancer was the (affect, effect) of Owen's 30-year smoking habit.
3. Abdi was not (allowed, aloud) to stay out after his curfew.
4. Jesse Owens and Carl Lewis (are, our) two of (are, our) most famous track-and-field athletes.
5. Without lotion, my skin feels (coarse, course).
6. We ate (desert, dessert) at a restaurant near the (desert, dessert) in Arizona.
7. Dzuy jogs a little (farther, further) down the road every day.
8. I only listened to the (later, latter) part of his speech because I was daydreaming during the first part.
9. If the coach had not paced back and (forth, fourth), yelling and screaming, the Hainesville Hounds may have won their (forth, fourth) football game of the season.
10. There will be no (peace, piece) in my house until Crystal finds the (peace, piece) of the puzzle that she hid.
11. (Then, Than) Pete Samparas made up his mind to become a better tennis player (then, than) any other player in the world.
12. Her (role, roll) in the play had her eating a dinner (role, roll) and saying to the audience: "Mmmm, that tastes great!"

Name ______________________ Date ______________

134. The Spelling Crossword

The clues for the crossword are misspelled words. Spell these words correctly in the appropriate place in the crossword.

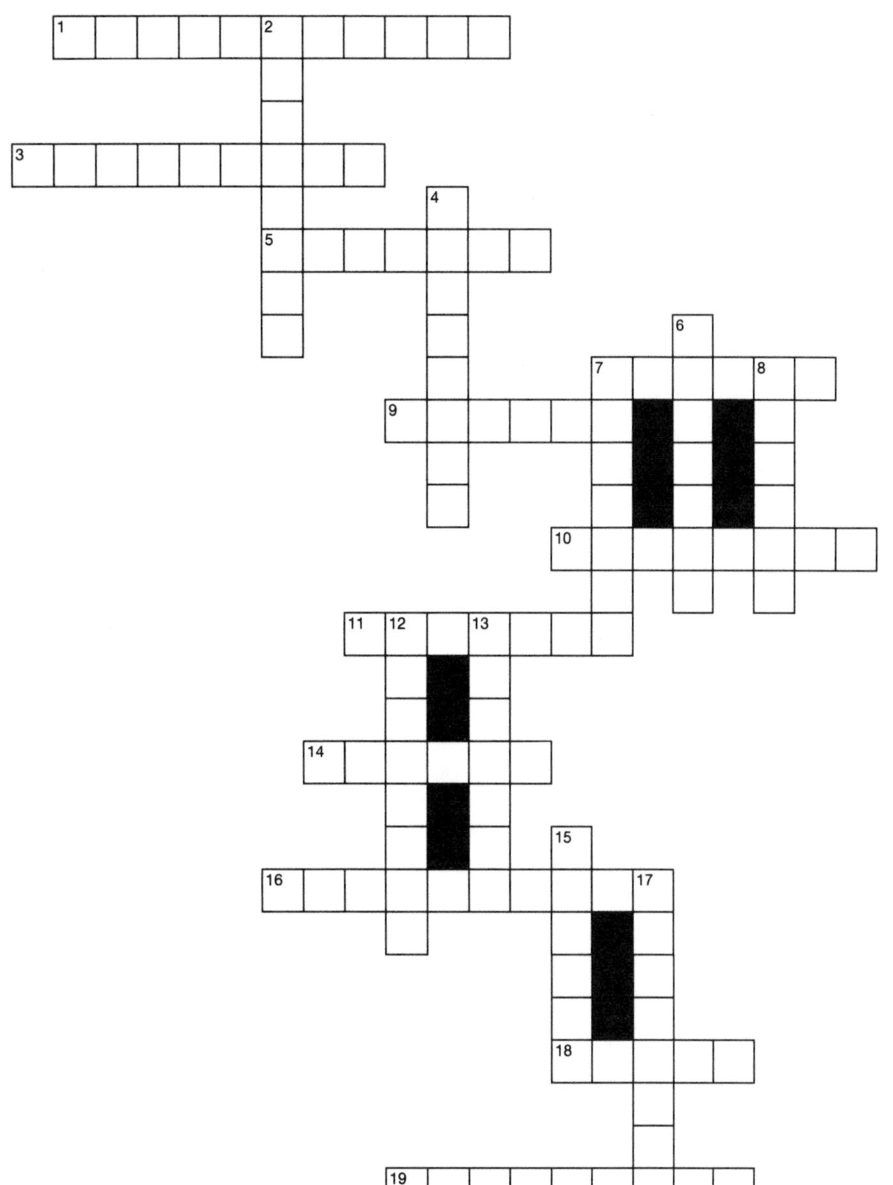

Across

1. contraversy
3. interupt
5. recieve
7. artic
9. victam
10. febuary
11. dispair
14. Agust
16. adolesent
18. theif
19. sincerly

Down

2. occured
4. mischeif
6. aquire
7. amature
8. Indain
12. eligable
13. posess
15. hieght
17. teribile

Name ______________________________ Date ____________________

135. The Spelling Bee

The students listed below have been involved in a spelling bee. In Round One, each student was given a different word to spell. On this page, we are given both the word and the student's attempt to spell the word. Which students succeed in advancing to Round Two? Help the students who did not advance by teaching them how to spell their word by correctly spelling the word in the space provided.

1. Xavier's word—*recommend* ______________________________
2. Seward's word—*excitement* ______________________________
3. Edwina's word—*prestidge* ______________________________
4. Priscilla's word—*arguement* ______________________________
5. Austin's word—*develope* ______________________________
6. Brett's word—*principle* ______________________________
7. Veronica's word—*arrangment* ______________________________
8. Noelle's word—permitted ______________________________
9. Byron's word—condemm ______________________________
10. Thelma's word—occassion ______________________________
11. Darian's word—untill ______________________________
12. Fiona's word—stoped ______________________________
13. Ruth's word—picnicking ______________________________
14. Tristan's word—marriage ______________________________
15. Cole's word—guard ______________________________

Which students made Round Two?

____

____

____

Name ______________________________ Date ____________________

136. Spelling Activity

Circle the letter beside the correctly spelled words below and correct the misspelled words. Unscramble the circled letters to find a good way to spend your leisure time.

A) SUBTLE ______________________________

B) COMFORTIBLE ______________________________

C) UNFORTUNATLY ______________________________

D) IMPOSSIBLE ______________________________

E) RESPONSIBLE ______________________________

F) PREFERED ______________________________

G) MISCHIEVOUS ______________________________

H) PREVELENT ______________________________

I) HYPOCRITE ______________________________

J) CONCIEVE ______________________________

K) ANNUALY ______________________________

L) APPOLOGY ______________________________

M) SIEZE ______________________________

N) YIELD ______________________________

O) TRADGIC ______________________________

P) FEIRCE ______________________________

Q) FACINATE ______________________________

R) NECESSARY ______________________________

S) SCHEDUAL ______________________________

T) MINITURE ______________________________

U) FEBUARY ______________________________

V) EXPECIALY ______________________________

W) GULTY ______________________________

X) HAPPENED ______________________________

Y) HAVEING ______________________________

Z) PICNICING ______________________________

A good way to spend your leisure time: ______________________________

Name ______________________________ Date ____________________

137. Spelling Demons

Circle the word in each row that is spelled correctly.

For example:

begining	(beginning)	beggining
1. acknowledgment	acknowledgement	acknowledgemant
2. hinderance	hindrence	hindrance
3. supercede	supersede	supersead
4. villian	villain	villan
5. grammer	gramer	grammar
6. representative	representitive	representatif
7. embarass	embarras	embarrass
8. preceed	precede	preseed
9. exaggerate	exagerate	exageraite
10. definitely	definately	definatly
11. calendar	calandar	calender
12. stuborn	stubburn	stubborn
13. vegatable	vegetable	vegetible
14. accomodate	accommodate	accommadate
15. ocassionally	occassionally	occasionally
16. judgement	judjment	judgment

Name ______________________________ Date ____________________

138. Which One Belongs?

Only ONE word is spelled correctly in each group of words. Circle the correctly spelled word and correct the misspelled words in the spaces.

Group 1

cafetria ____________________

labratory ____________________

library ____________________

mathamatics ____________________

Group 2

goverment ____________________

principal ____________________

polition ____________________

proffessor ____________________

Group 3

different ____________________

continualy ____________________

incredable ____________________

perpare ____________________

Group 4

absense ____________________

beleif ____________________

couragous ____________________

dependent ____________________

Group 5

hunderd (100) ____________________

forth (4th) ____________________

eighth (8th) ____________________

eleventh (11th) ____________________

Group 6

imaginery ____________________

literature ____________________

knowladge ____________________

writen ____________________

Group 7

payed ____________________

tryed ____________________

answered ____________________

perfered ____________________

Group 8

disasterous ____________________

extrordinary ____________________

awful ____________________

magnificant ____________________

Name ______________________________ Date ____________________

139. Spelling Maze I

Shade in the boxes with the words that are spelled correctly in order to find the pathway through the maze. Correct the misspelled words on the lines below.

\ ENTER / \ EXIT /

believe	usually	proffessional	finnally	obise	amateur
alot	ridicule	genious	inpatiant	viewed	especially
visites	grammar	destroy	garantee	excellent	luckly
victom	possitive	require	wich	using	aproximate
commited	agression	occurred	among	freezer	suseptible
negitive	lazyness	appearence	easyer	unfortunatly	embarras
wether	recieve	vegatate	intelectual	miscariage	perscribe

Name ______________________ Date ______________

140. Spelling Maze II

Shade in the boxes with the words that are spelled correctly in order to find the pathway through the maze. Correct the misspelled words on the lines below.

jelousy	favour	tried	luxury	neighbor	definately
extremly	enviroment	intelligence	vacumm	omitted	attendance
surprize	disipline	prominent	vengance	sincerly	twelth
cemetery	committee	dilemma	absense	nonsence	recieve
arguing	occurance	couragous	benefitted	awfull	guidence
separate	noticeable	ignorant	criticise	bullatin	runing
sking	writting	exhibit	immediatly	lisence	rythm

/ EXIT \

\ ENTER /

Name ______________________________ Date ____________________

141. Dot-to-Dot Spelling

If a word in the list below is spelled correctly, then connect the dots between the number beside the *correctly* spelled word and the number beside the *next* correctly spelled word. If the word is not spelled correctly, make the necessary corrections in the space next to the word. What do the connected dots make?

1. shriek ______________
2. similar ______________
3. trys ______________
4. eligable ______________
5. leisure ______________
6. particular ______________
7. expense ______________
8. conscious ______________
9. Britain ______________
10. realy ______________
11. familar ______________
12. ordinary ______________
13. miscellaneous ______________
14. pleasent ______________
15. judgment ______________
16. individual ______________
17. preformance ______________
18. generaly ______________

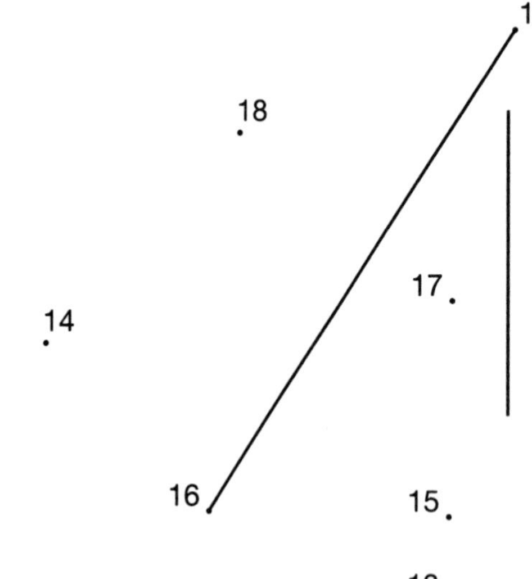

Name ______________________________ Date ________________

142. The Canadian Way

Although many Canadians speak English, they often spell words differently from Americans. In the chart below are words that are spelled correctly in Canada. If they are also spelled correctly in America, shade the box with the correctly spelled word. If the spelling of the word is different from that in America, do not shade the box but correctly spell the word on one of the lines below.

When you are finished, the shaded area will reveal a saying for which Canadians are famous.

profession	cereal	labour	valuable	cheque	hesitate
doubt	travelling	counsellor	weigh	centre	saucer
medicine	relief	defence	usually	evidently	perhaps
occurring	honour	levelled	ancient	neighbour	importance
innocent	remember	litre	aisle	favourite	suppose

__________ __________ __________

__________ __________ __________

__________ __________ __________

__________ __________ __________

__________ __________ __________

__________ __________ __________

__________ __________ __________

__________ __________ __________

Name ______________________________ Date ____________________

143. The Menu

There are 20 spelling mistakes in this menu. Circle each error and write the correctly spelled words on the lines below.

Dougs Resturant

Apetisers

Tomatoe Soup
Vegable Tray
Ceaser Salad

Main Coarses

Steak and Kidny Pie
Chicken Fahitas
Brocolli and Beef Caseroll
Veal Pamresean and Sweet Potatos
Lazanya and Salad
Spagetti and Meatballs

Deserts

Cinamin Rolls
Chocalate Chip Cookies

Beveroges

Soda, Cofee, Tea and Milkshakes

____________________ ____________________ ____________________

____________________ ____________________ ____________________

____________________ ____________________ ____________________

____________________ ____________________ ____________________

____________________ ____________________ ____________________

____________________ ____________________ ____________________

____________________ ____________________ ____________________

Name ______________________ Date ______________

144. The Job Application

Waldo recently graduated with a marketing diploma, and is now sending his résumé and cover letter to a number of marketing departments in major American companies. Unfortunately, Waldo has misspelled the name of every company in his cover letters. Fortunately, as Waldo's friend, you noticed the mistakes before he mailed the résumés. Help Waldo by correcting the spelling of each American company in the space provided.

1. Johnston & Johnston ______________________
2. Procter and Gambel ______________________
3. Genoral Moters ______________________
4. Wallmart ______________________
5. Hewlet-Pakard ______________________
6. Home Depote ______________________
7. Texoco ______________________
8. JC Penny ______________________
9. Gilete ______________________
10. Macdonalds ______________________
11. Alstate ______________________
12. Metrapolitian Life Insuronce ______________________

Name ______________________________ Date ________________

145. Spelling States

Many of the states below are misspelled. Correct the ones that are misspelled and circle the correctly spelled ones.

Alobama
Alaska
Arizona
Arkansa
California
Colarado
Conneticut
Deloware
Florida
Georga
Hawai
Idaho

Illenois
Indana
Iowa
Kansas
Kentuky
Lousiana
Maine
Mariland
Massachusettes
Michigon
Minnisota
Missisippi
Missori

Montona
Nebrasca
Neveda
New Hamshire
New Jersy
New Mexico
New York
North Caralina
North Dakota
Ohio
Oklahama
Oreogon
Pensylvanea

Road Island
South Carlina
South Dakota
Tenesee
Texus
Uta
Vermant
Virgina
Washingten
West Virgina
Wisconsine
Woming

Name ______________________ Date ______________

146. A+ Spelling

The words below all start with *A*. Using the clues that are given, determine each word. *Example:*
A + 2 letters = to assist ______aid______

1. A + 1 letter = indefinite article ______________
2. A + 2 letters = playing card ______________
3. A + 2 letters = gorilla ______________
4. A + 2 letters = past tense of eat ______________
5. A + 3 letters = partly open ______________
6. A + 3 letters = not an uncle ______________
7. A + 3 letters = pimples ______________
8. A + 4 letters = to enter ______________
9. A + 4 letters = to fight or debate ______________
10. A + 4 letters = opposite of dead ______________
11. A + 4 letters = not asleep ______________
12. A + 5 letters = the 8th month ______________
13. A + 5 letters = fall season ______________
14. A + 6 letters = a public sale with bids ______________
15. A + 6 letters = a branch of mathematics ______________
16. A + 6 letters = USA ______________
17. A + 7 letters = a starvation disease ______________
18. A + 8 letters = large reptile ______________
19. A + 8 letters = one's signature ______________
20. A + 8 letters = an unknown person ______________

Name ______________________________ Date ________________

147. B+ Spelling

These words all start with *B*. Using the clues that are given, determine what the word is. *Example:*
B + 2 letters = the opposite of good ______bad______

1. B + 1 letter = a word that rhymes with *me* and means *am* ______________
2. B + 2 letters = the opposite of girl ______________
3. B + 2 letters = present tense of bought ______________
4. B + 3 letters = hold up pants ______________
5. B + 3 letters = color of the sky ______________
6. B + 3 letters = a male cow ______________
7. B + 4 letters = the person marrying the groom ______________
8. B + 4 letters = unable to see ______________
9. B + 4 letters = stringed instrument like a guitar ______________
10. B + 5 letters = a sport where people fight with fists ______________
11. B + 5 letters = limb of a tree ______________
12. B + 6 letters = a bunch of flowers ______________
13. B + 6 letters = the opposite of sister ______________
14. B + 6 letters = covers a wound ______________
15. B + 6 letters = a person who sells meat ______________
16. B + 6 letters = a type of science ______________
17. B + 7 letters = a one-story house ______________
18. B + 7 letters = everyone celebrates one a year ______________
19. B + 8 letters = a racket sport ______________
20. B + 8 letters = opposite of end ______________

Name ______________________ Date ______________

148. The Spelling Hexagon

Spell as many words as you can by starting anywhere on the diagram and moving along the connecting lines. Do not skip letters. You may come back and use a letter again, but do not use a letter twice in succession. For example, it is possible to spell the word *nun*, but you may not spell the word *noon.*

One point	=	each three-letter word
Two points	=	each four-letter word
Three points	=	each five-letter word
Four points	=	each six+-letter word

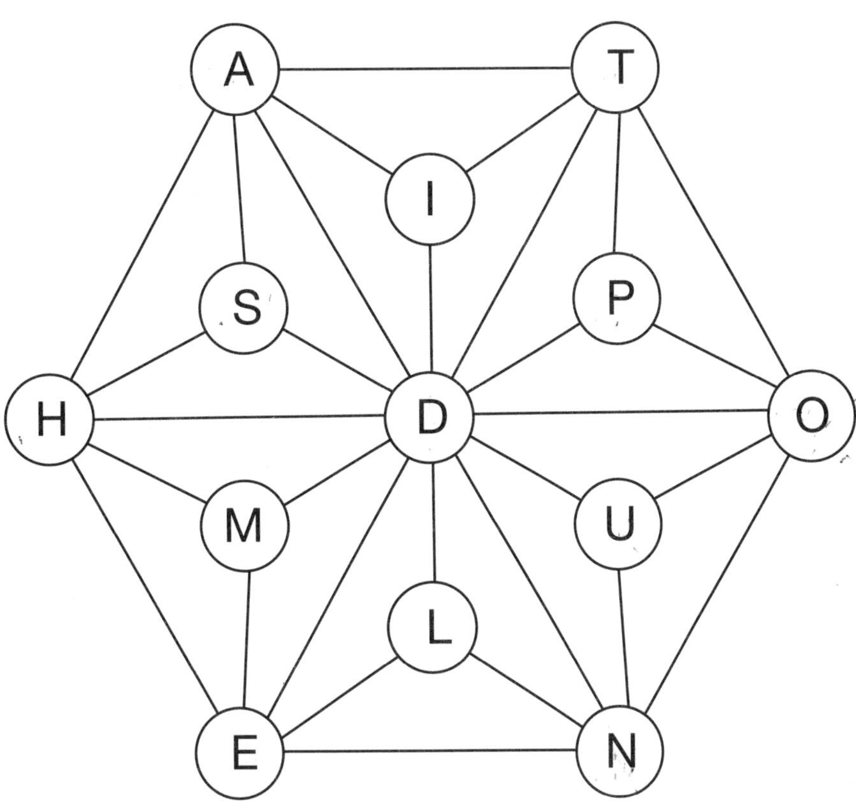

3-letter words	4-letter words	5-letter words	6+-letter words

Name ______________________________ Date ____________________

149. The Spelling Box

Spell as many words as you can. Start anywhere in the box and move up, down, or diagonally. You may reuse a letter but not twice in succession. For example, you can spell *none,* but you cannot spell *noon.* Do not use short forms or acronyms. How many words can you find?

B	T	P	L
E	S	A	I
Y	E	S	R
M	O	N	G

Section 6

VOCABULARY AND WORD BUILDING

"'When I use a word,' Humpty Dumpty said, in a rather scornful tone, 'it means just what I choose it to mean—neither more nor less.'"

LEWIS CARROLL

Name ______________________ Date ______________

150. Denotation and Connotation

Every word has both a denotative meaning and a connotative meaning. The denotation is the specific and exact meaning of a word. The connotation of a word is the emotional association that word holds for individuals or groups. For example, according to *Webster's Dictionary,* the denotative meaning of the word *cool* is "to lose heat or warmth." However, one of the connotative meanings of the word *cool* is "having self-confidence, being a relaxed and popular person."

For each word in the chart, come up with denotative and connotative definitions.

Word	Denotative Definition	Connotative Definition
Mother		
Home		
School		
Love		
Television		

Name ____________________ Date ____________

151. Word Wheels

Using each of the six roots in the middle wheel, create as many words as possible taking the prefixes and/or suffixes from the outer wheels.

Prefixes

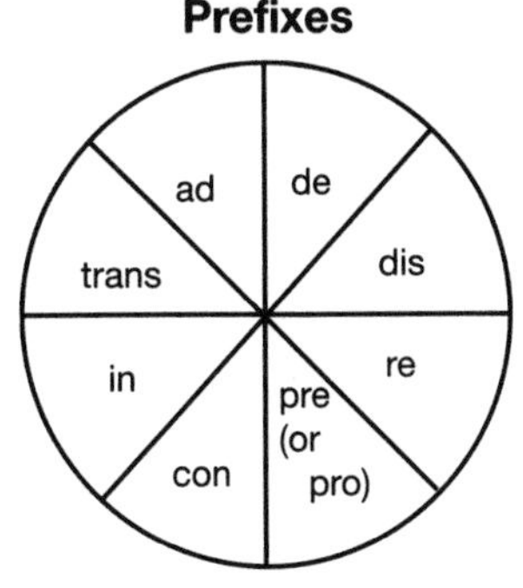

Roots

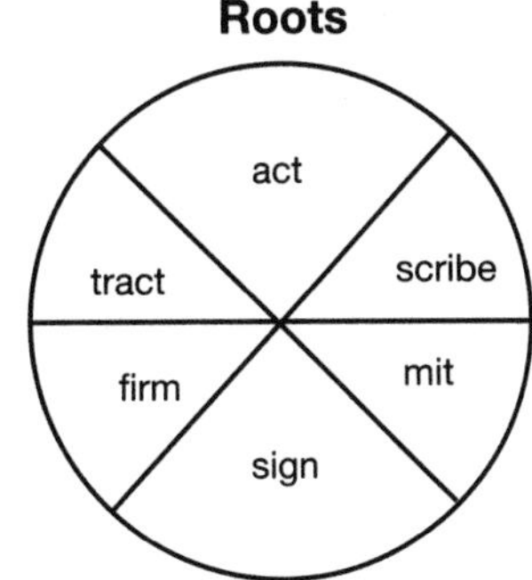

Suffixes

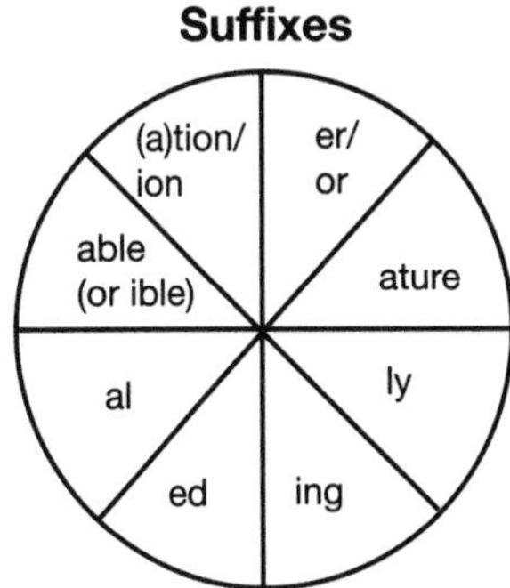

______	______	______
______	______	______
______	______	______
______	______	______
______	______	______
______	______	______
______	______	______
______	______	______
______	______	______
______	______	______
______	______	______
______	______	______
______	______	______
______	______	______
______	______	______
______	______	______
______	______	______

Name ______________________________ Date ____________________

152. Four-Letter Word Fun

Create as many four-letter words as you can by first using a letter from the circle in the center. Then pick the second letter from the circle next to the center circle and so on. You must move from the center circle out.

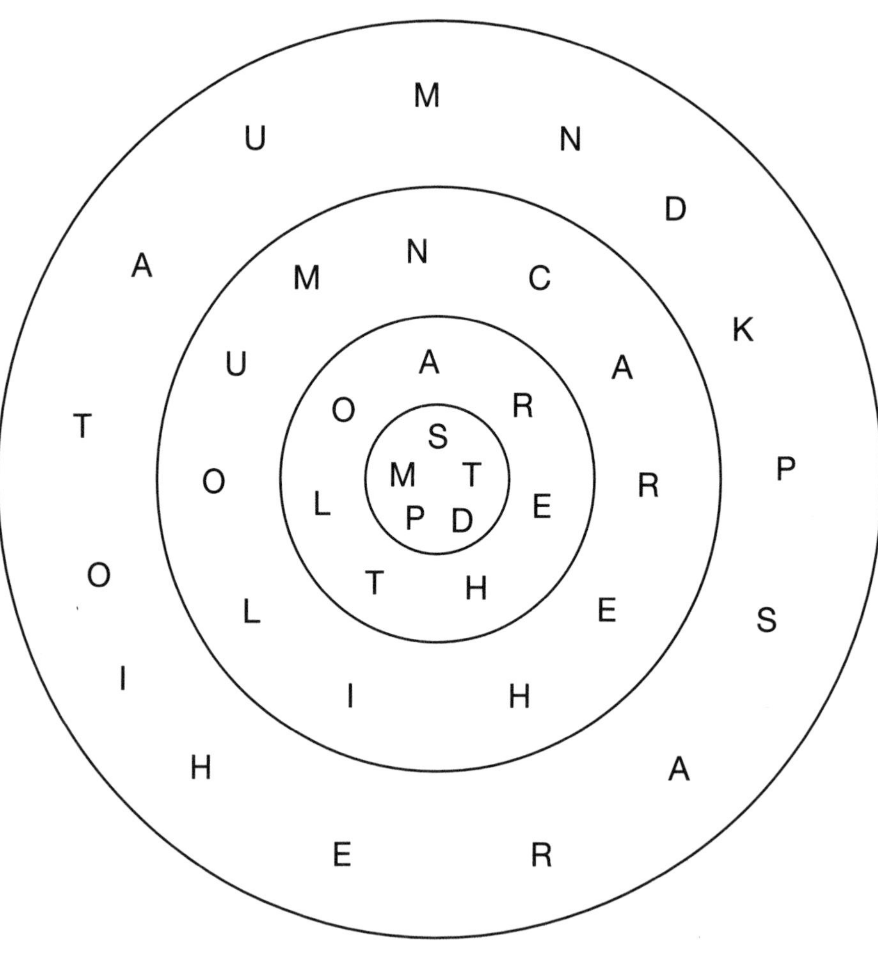

_______________ _______________ _______________

_______________ _______________ _______________

_______________ _______________ _______________

_______________ _______________ _______________

_______________ _______________ _______________

_______________ _______________ _______________

_______________ _______________ _______________

Name ______________________ Date ______________

153. Rhyming Wheels

The ending of a word is in the middle of each circle. In the spokes of the circle write as many words as you can that rhyme with that ending. For example:

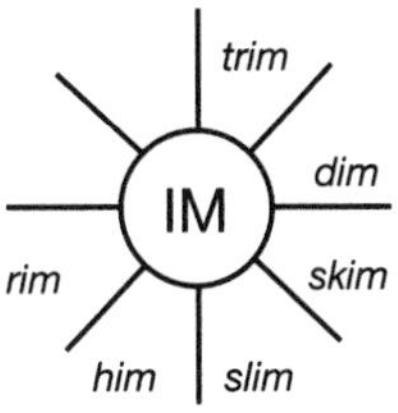

IM
trim
dim
skim
slim
him
rim

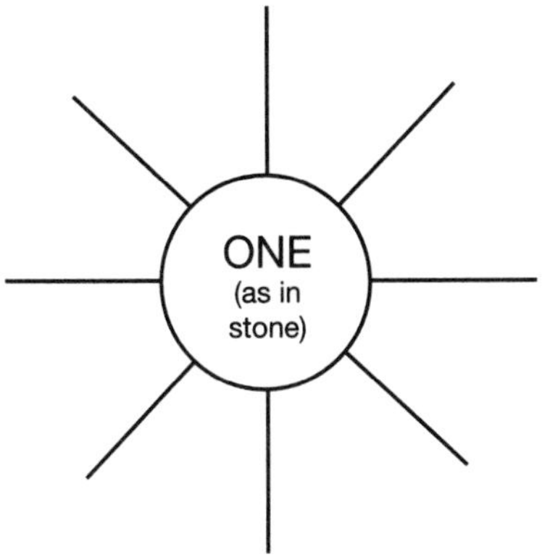

ONE
(as in stone)

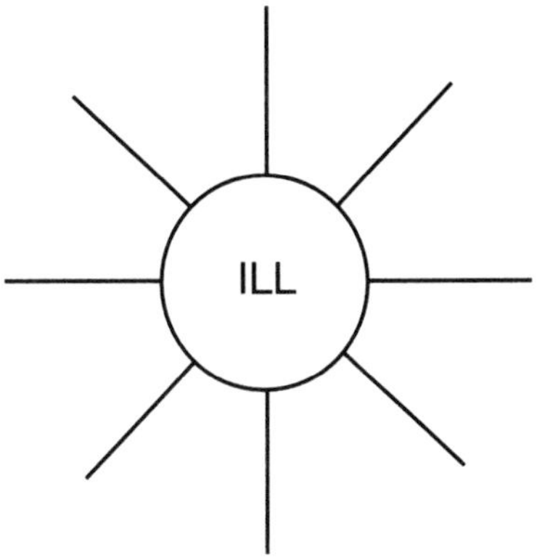

ILL

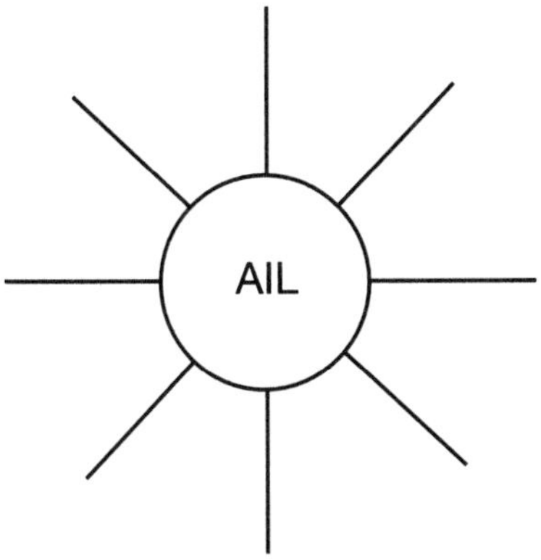

AIL

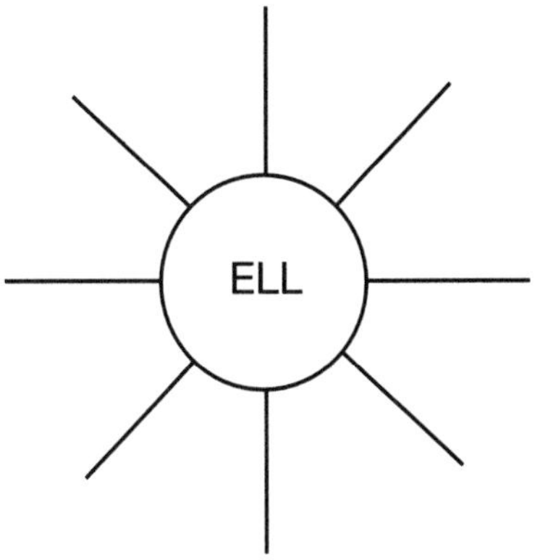

ELL

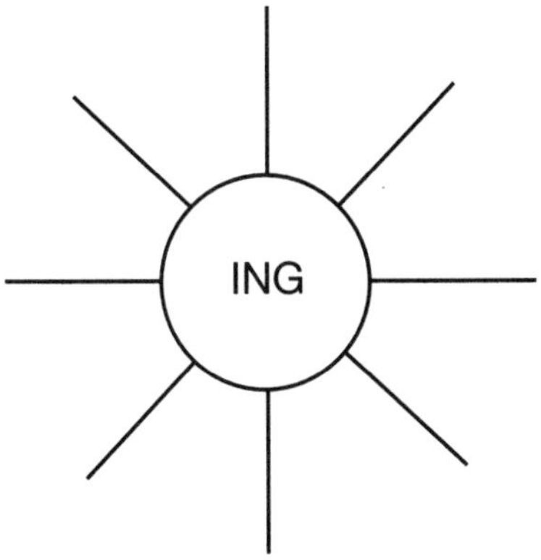

ING

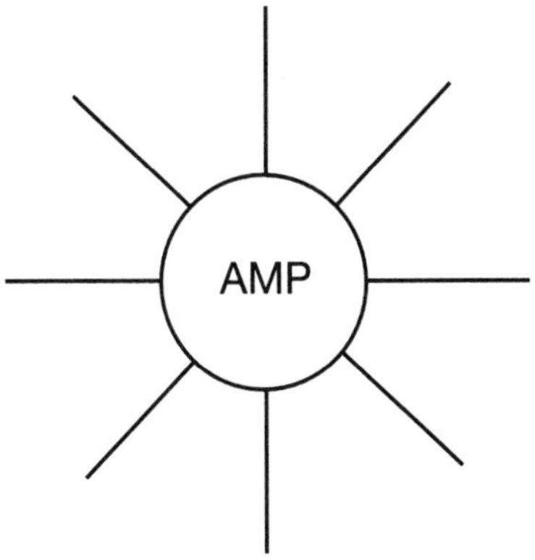

AMP

Name ______________________________ Date ________________

154. Creating "Sub" Words

The prefix "sub" means: 1. under, beneath, below; 2. almost, nearly, or slightly; 3. lower in rank or grade. Using the prefix "sub," complete the word clustering with examples of words that come from this prefix.

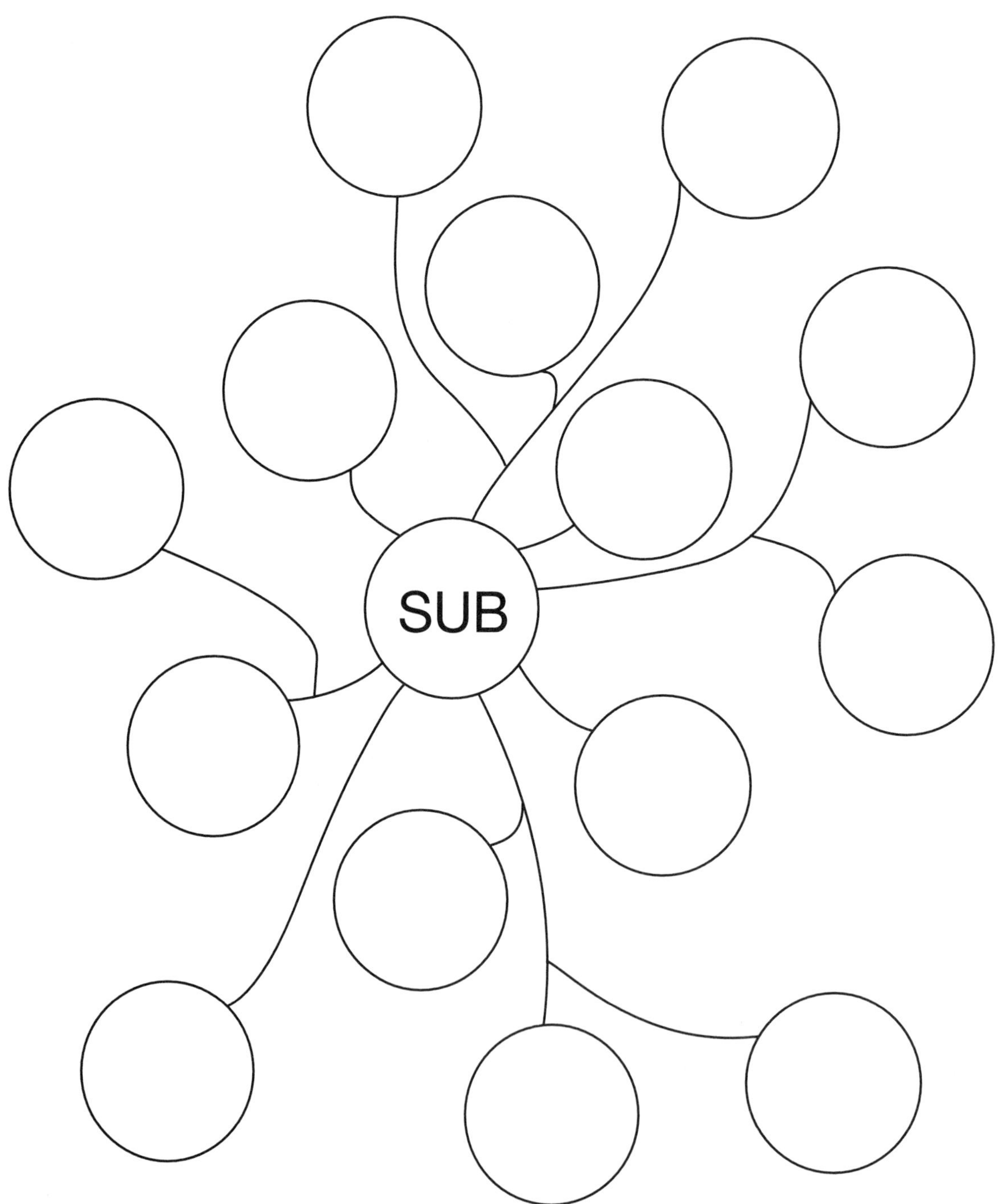

Name ______________________________ Date ____________________

155. Creating "Port" Words

The root word "port" means to carry. Using "port" as the root, complete the word clustering with as many words as possible deriving from the root.

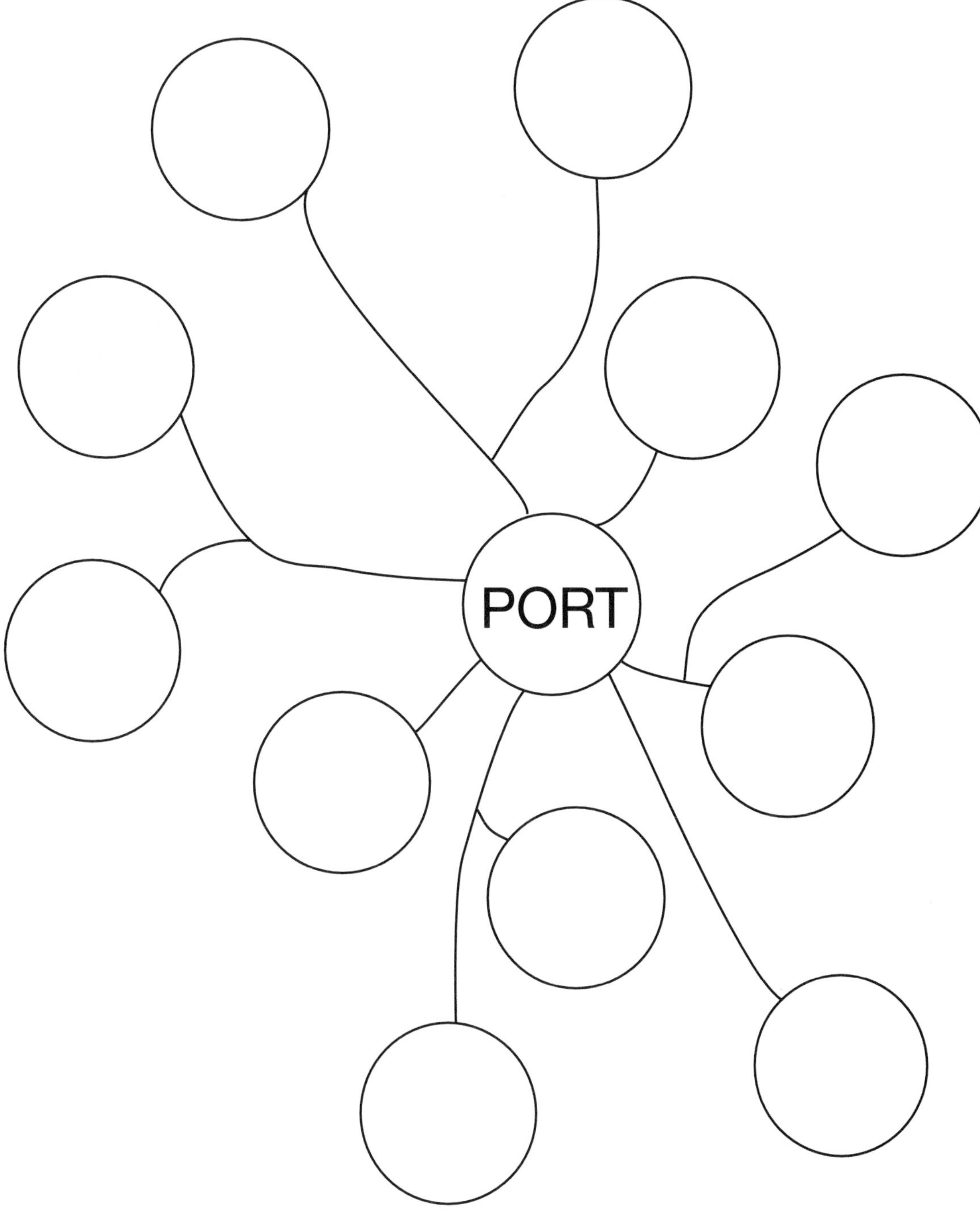

Name ______________________________ Date ____________________

156. Word Pyramids

Each pyramid has a letter at the top. In each space below, create a word that begins with the letter at the top of the pyramid. (If there are 2 spaces, create a 2-letter word, etc.) Here is a sample done for you:

O
ON
OLD
ONCE
OUNCE

A

___ ___

___ ___ ___

___ ___ ___ ___

___ ___ ___ ___ ___

___ ___ ___ ___ ___ ___

S

___ ___

___ ___ ___

___ ___ ___ ___

___ ___ ___ ___ ___

___ ___ ___ ___ ___ ___

T

___ ___

___ ___ ___

___ ___ ___ ___

___ ___ ___ ___ ___

___ ___ ___ ___ ___ ___

D

___ ___

___ ___ ___

___ ___ ___ ___

___ ___ ___ ___ ___

___ ___ ___ ___ ___ ___

Name ______________________________ Date ____________________

157. Magic Squares: E Words

Select the corresponding "E" word from among the numbered definitions. Write the number in the appropriate box in the magic square below. The sum of the numbers will be the same across each row and down each column. This sum is the magic number.

E Words	Definitions
(A) EDIBLE	(1) No longer existing
(B) EFFICIENT	(2) Productive with minimum waste of effort
(C) ELABORATE	(3) Highly developed or complicated
(D) ELDER	(4) Necessary, indispensable
(E) ELEMENTARY	(5) Dealing with the simplest facts of a subject
(F) ELEVATE	(6) To put stress on
(G) ELIGIBLE	(7) To preserve from decay
(H) ELIMINATE	(8) Remove or get rid of
(I) ELITE	(9) Select group or class
(J) EMBALM	(10) Entitled to be chosen for
(K) EMPHASIZE	(11) Raise or lift up
(L) ENORMITY	(12) Serious error or monstrous wickedness
(M) ESSENTIAL	(13) A senior or person of greater age
(N) EVACUATE	(14) Send people away from a place of danger
(O) EXAGGERATE	(15) To make a thing seem larger or greater than it really is
(P) EXTINCT	(16) To be eaten

THE MAGIC SQUARE

A	B	C	D
E	F	G	H
I	J	K	L
M	N	O	P

THE MAGIC NUMBER IS ________

Name ______________________________ Date ____________________

158. Improve Your Vocabulary

Match the words in the box with their definitions below.

1. Disparity	6. Nebulous	11. Solemnity
2. Eccentric	7. Ostentation	12. Surreptitious
3. Enigmatic	8. Pessimistic	13. Ubiquitous
4. Fastidious	9. Prodigious	14. Valiant
5. Malevolent	10. Proprietor	15. Perfunctory

_____ Mysterious or obscure

_____ Enormous or extraordinary in size, quality or degree; abnormal

_____ Vague or confused; cloud-like, hazy

_____ Formal, dignified

_____ Strong and courageous

_____ A person having exclusive title to something; an owner

_____ Present everywhere or in several places simultaneously

_____ Wishing evil toward others

_____ Acting in a secret manner; sly

_____ Unconventional in appearance or behavior

_____ Excessive exhibition; showiness

_____ Negative or cynical in outlook

_____ Exceedingly delicate or refined; overly nice; squeamish

_____ Mechanical or superficial, careless in approach

_____ Inequality, difference; lack of similarity, as in age or rank

Name ______________________________ Date ____________________

159. Multiple-Choice Vocabulary

Circle the correct definition for each word.

1. ACCEPT
   a. exclude from
   b. receive
   c. deliver
   d. rule out

2. REFERENDUM
   a. An election in third-world countries.
   b. The formal name of any meeting between the President and Vice President.
   c. The submission of a proposed law to a popular vote.
   d. When there is a need for a second vote.

3. DEJECTION
   a. depression
   b. rejection
   c. go away
   d. marriage break-up

4. BILINGUAL
   a. lover of words
   b. citizen of two countries
   c. unable to speak
   d. able to speak two languages

5. IDIOSYNCRASY
   a. personal oddity
   b. mentally-challenged person
   c. stranger to a group
   d. group of co-workers

6. CHATELAINE
   a. small castle
   b. mistress of a large house
   c. pond
   d. name of a Spanish dance

Name ________________________________ Date ____________________

160. Other Words

Each sentence has one word underlined. In the space provided, write another word(s) that means the same as the underlined word and could, therefore, be substituted for that word in the sentence.

1. Last weekend our forty-year-old cousin shocked the family by marrying an <u>octogenarian</u>.

____

2. My <u>fastidious</u> uncle always lined up his collection of soldiers in perfect rows.

____

3. Our state prison is full of my relatives who are <u>malefactors</u>.

____

4. Josie planned to move to New York and become a <u>thespian</u>.

____

5. For his part in history, Adolph Hitler could be called a <u>genocidal</u> maniac.

____

6. Having a grandfather clock and a baby grand piano in the summer cottage made the cottage quite <u>grandiose</u>.

____

7. It was <u>illuminating</u> for Charles when he finally understood the math equation.

____

8. Eduardo's grandmother was in a <u>juvenescence</u> mood when she acquired a motorcycle and a leather jacket.

____

9. My friend showed a <u>nefarious</u> side of her personality when she slyly attempted to break up my boyfriend and me.

____

10. I was always considered an <u>INTROVERT</u> because I hated going out in crowds.

____

Name ______________________________ Date ____________________

161. A Letter

An adoring grandfather wrote this humorous letter to his one-year-old grandson. Some of the words are far too difficult for a child to read. For each word underlined, think of another word that means the same but is easier to understand and write it above the underlined word.

Sir:

It is indeed an honor and privilege to address you on this auspicious occasion and to extend my felicitations and congratulations to you on reaching the venerable age of ONE.

Few of us can boast of such a prodigious amount of youth. Thousands of influences, ambitions, pleasures, and sorrows are beckoning you in the long line of years (yet how short they become in retrospect). It is my ardent hope that your guardian angel will see that the years are filled with happiness in abundance but sorrows will be of no consequence. Your adoring grandma has bought a gift for you to commemorate this occasion.

I know you will read every word of this letter and ponder over it, so I will not encroach on your time by writing at length.

With every good wish I am proud to subscribe myself,

Your loving grandpappy

Name ______________________________ Date ____________________

162. An Antonym Box

Antonyms are two words with opposite meanings (e.g., love/hate). For each word, write the antonym in the corresponding crossword. The last letter of the first word forms the first letter of the next word.

ACROSS

1. INTERIOR
2. WRONG
3. UNGRATEFUL
9. RIGHT
10. VERTICAL
11. LIFE
12. BEGINNING

DOWN

1. LATENESS
4. DARK
5. WIDE
6. OLD
7. LOSER
8. ACCEPT
13. LOVE
14. LOW
15. ROUGH

Name ______________________ Date ______________

163. Another Antonym Box

Antonyms are two words with opposite meanings (e.g., love/hate). For each word, write the antonym in the corresponding crossword. The last letter of the first word forms the first letter of the next word.

ACROSS

1. OUTSIDE
2. GOOD
3. RIGHT
4. FALSE
10. WIN
11. SHORT
12. DAY
13. TEACH

DOWN

1. OUT
5. BEGINNING
6. UP
7. SOUTH
8. COLD
9. WILD
14. HEAD
15. ENTER
16. COMMON
17. UNDER
18. YES

Name ______________________________ Date ____________________

164. The Synonym Chart

Write synonyms for the following words. (A *synonym* is a word that has the same, or nearly the same, meaning as another word. *Giant* and *jumbo* are synonyms.)

WALK ____________ ____________ ____________

MONEY ____________ ____________ ____________

GOOD ____________ ____________ ____________

BEGINNING ____________ ____________ ____________

GOVERNMENT ____________ ____________ ____________

THANKFUL ____________ ____________ ____________

MUSIC ____________ ____________ ____________

RAIN ____________ ____________ ____________

COLD ____________ ____________ ____________

LIGHT ____________ ____________ ____________

TALK ____________ ____________ ____________

TEST ____________ ____________ ____________

RICH ____________ ____________ ____________

SLEEP ____________ ____________ ____________

PRISON ____________ ____________ ____________

STOP ____________ ____________ ____________

MOUNTAIN ____________ ____________ ____________

LANGUAGE ____________ ____________ ____________

POOR ____________ ____________ ____________

VACATION ____________ ____________ ____________

Name ______________________ Date ______________

165. A Synonym Box

Synonyms are two words with the same, or similar, meaning (e.g., large/huge). For each word, write its synonym in the corresponding crossword. The last letter of the first word forms the first letter of the next word.

1 2 3 4

15

ACROSS

1. TINY
2. FATAL
3. FREEDOM
9. PERISH
10. BEGINNER
11. JOURNEY

DOWN

1. TRAP
4. PEST
5. DEPART
6. ALSO
7. STRANGE
8. SLOW
12. CHURCH
13. QUIET
14. AGREED
15. JEALOUS

14 5

13 6

7

12 8

11 10 9

Name ______________________ Date ______________

166. Another Synonym Box

Synonyms are two words with the same, or similar, meaning (e.g., large/huge). For each word, write its synonym in the corresponding crossword. The last letter of the first word forms the first letter of the next word.

ACROSS

1. DOWNPOUR
2. FILM
3. WORLD
4. CAP
10. LEAP
11. WEALTHY
12. TERROR
13. PIXIE
14. POND
15. BAD
16. PASTRY

DOWN

1. KIN
5. DITCH
6. INN
7. GRASS
8. COUNTRY
9. SLEEP
17. FAUCET
18. LAMP
19. SATAN
20. FINISH

Name ______________________________ Date ____________________

167. Career Jargon

Each career has its own jargon or slang. People in certain careers use words every day that may not be understandable to people outside those careers. Below are several careers followed by a list of words. Which word goes with the career? Circle the correct word. You may want to use a dictionary.

1. Career: FLORIST
   a. Begonia
   b. Noetic
   c. Patina

2. Career: ARTIST
   a. Lithograph
   b. Cogitate
   c. Ethos

3. Career: DENTIST
   a. Flotation
   b. Fluoridate
   c. Flounce

4. Career: MARINE
   a. Practical
   b. Tactical
   c. Nautical

5. Career: FARMER
   a. Heifer
   b. Bravura
   c. Linoleum

6. Career: MINISTER
   a. Sequoia
   b. Ungulate
   c. Benediction

7. Career: LAWYER
   a. Lampoon
   b. Litigation
   c. Lisle

8. Career: MUSICIAN
   a. All'ottava
   b. Amalgam
   c. Anesthetic

9. Career: BAKER
   a. Mead
   b. Steed
   c. Knead

10. Career: PROFESSOR
    a. Tenuous
    b. Tenure
    c. Tensile

Name ____________________ Date ____________

168. Ology Vocabulary

The suffix *ology* means "the science of" or "the study of." Match each word in Column A with the correct word in Column B.

<u>Column A</u> (the ology word)	<u>Column B</u> (the study of . . .)
ANTHROPOLOGY	Heart
ARCHAEOLOGY	Nerves (the nervous system)
CARDIOLOGY	Fruit
ETYMOLOGY	Reptiles
GEOLOGY	Human (Culture)
GYNECOLOGY	Earthquakes
HERPETOLOGY	Women
METEOROLOGY	Ancient People
NEUROLOGY	Fossils
ORNITHOLOGY	Weather
PALEONTOLOGY	Word Origins
POMOLOGY	God
PSYCHOLOGY	Animals
SEISMOLOGY	Birds
THEOLOGY	Mind
ZOOLOGY	Earth

Name ________________________________ Date ____________________

169. What Do They Fear?

The word *phobia* means fear. *Phobia* is the root of the words below. Each of these words means fear of something. Try to match the things people fear by connecting the word in Column A to what is feared in Column B.

Column A	Column B
AEROPHOBIA	Fear of Thunder
ARACHNOPHOBIA	Fear of Mice
BRONTOPHOBIA	Fear of Dogs
CLAUSTROPHOBIA	Fear of Being Bored
CYNOPHOBIA	Fear of Snakes
GERONTOPHOBIA	Fear of Flying
HEMOPHOBIA	Fear of Speaking Aloud
MIKROPHOBIA	Fear of Numbers
MUROPHOBIA	Fear of Germs
NUMEROPHOBIA	Fear of Closed Spaces
OPHIDIOPHOBIA	Fear of Strangers
PHONOPHOBIA	Fear of Blood
THAASOPHOBIA	Fear of the Number 13
TRISKAIDEKAPHOBIA	Fear of Spiders
XENOPHOBIA	Fear of Old Age

Name ______________________________ Date ____________________

170. Which Word Doesn't Belong (Part I)

In each group below, three of the words have similar meanings while a fourth word means something completely different.

For example:

MONOTONOUS
BANAL
FACETIOUS
PLATITUDINOUS

In this example, *facetious* does not fit. The other three words mean dull, flat, or boring. *Facetious* is different because it refers to flippant or sarcastic humor.

In each group, which word does not belong? *Helpful hint:* You may wish to use a dictionary.

Group 1

LOQUACIOUS
TACITURN
VERBOSITY
GARRULOUS

Group 2

DEFICIENT
BLEMISHED
IMPECCABLE
MARRED

Group 3

AFFRAY
BELLIGERENT
PUGNACIOUS
BENEVOLENT

Group 4

ANTAGONISM
CONTRADICTION
OPPOSITION
COOPERATION

Group 5

VERACITY
FRAUDULENCE
GUILE
DECEPTIVENESS

Group 6

OSCILLATE
FLUCTUATE
CERTITUDE
HESITATE

Group 7

PERFIDIOUS
INSIDIOUS
TREACHEROUS
SCRUPULOUS

Group 8

ILLUSTRIOUS
DISREPUTABLE
OPPROBRIOUS
DEROGATORY

Group 9

RELINQUISHMENT
TENANCY
ABDICATION
SURRENDER

Name ______________________________ Date ______________

171. Which Word Doesn't Belong? (Part II)

In each group below, three words have similar meanings while a fourth word means something completely different.

For example:

CORDIAL
ADVERSARY
AMICABLE
FRATERNIZE

In this example, *adversary* does not fit. The three other words mean friendly or making friends with. *Adversary* is different because it means an enemy or opponent.

In each group, which word does not belong? *Helpful hint:* You may wish to use a dictionary.

Group 1

AROMA
MALODOROUS
HALITOSIS
FETID

Group 2

FAINT
SWOON
FEIGN
COLLAPSE

Group 3

TRANSPARENT
TRANSLUCENT
TRANSMOGRIFY
TRANSPICIOUS

Group 4

PIXY
ELF
GNOME
TITAN

Group 5

MATERNAL
GREGARIOUS
FRATERNAL
AVUNCULAR

Group 6

IMPECUNIOUS
OPULENT
OSTENTATIOUS
AFFLUENT

Group 7

FLACCID
LIMP
FLABBY
FISSURE

Group 8

PLIABLE
FLEXIBLE
IMPERMEABLE
MALLEABLE

Group 9

PRURIENT
DISCREET
JUDICIOUS
PRUDENCE

Name ______________________________ Date __________________

172. Which Word Doesn't Belong? (Part III)

In each group below, three words have similar meanings while a fourth word means something completely different.

For example:

ARISTOCRATIC
PLEBIAN
UNREFINED
PROLETARIAN

In this example, *aristocratic* does not fit. The other three words refer to a person of a lower class, whereas the word *aristocratic* means a person has money and is stylish.

In each group, which word does not belong? *Helpful hint:* You may wish to use a dictionary.

Group 1

DOGMATIC
OPINIONATED
SUBMISSIVE
DICTATORIAL

Group 2

HARD-SHELL
HARD-LUCK
HARD-UP
HARD-DONE-BY

Group 3

NONPARTISAN
NONENTITY
UNCOMMITTED
DISINTERESTED

Group 4

OSTRACIZE
EXCLUDE
BANISH
ASSENT

Group 5

MALEVOLENT
MISANTHROPY
MAUDLIN
MALIGNITY

Group 6

APLOMB
SELF-CONFIDENT
ASSURED
ARCANE

Group 7

CONFUSE
POSTULANT
OBFUSCATE
BEWILDER

Group 8

AMEND
IMPROVE
AMBIVALENT
CORRECT

Group 9

UNFLAPPABLE
BAFFLE
PERPLEXED
NONPLUS

Section 7

LISTENING AND SPEAKING SKILLS

"'The time has come,' the Walrus said,
'to talk of many things:
Of shoes—and ships—a sealing wax—
Of cabbages—and kings—
And why the sea is boiling hot
And whether pigs have wings.'"

LEWIS CARROLL

173. First-Day Bingo

Get to know your classmates. How many different autographs can you get? Find someone who . . .

Has blue eyes	Can do a cartwheel	Plays football	Has an older sibling	Speaks a second language
Is wearing jeans	Is born in the same month as you	Has brown hair	Has a cat or a dog	Was born in another state
Has been to the Epcot Center in Florida	Has taken piano lessons	FREE SPACE	Loves to chat on the phone	Is wearing a necklace
Knows how to paddle a canoe	Is wearing green	Owns a computer	Has an autograph of a famous person	Has traveled outside of the U.S.A.
Is new to this school	Saw a movie on the weekend	Writes poetry or songs	Is wearing running shoes	Remembers the name of his/her first-grade teacher

Name ______________________________ Date ____________________

174. The Interview

This exercise will sharpen your listening, speaking, and writing skills. Pick a partner. (Try to pick a person you don't know well.) Ask your partner questions that will provide answers for the blanks below. After you have all your information, write a paragraph about your partner. After you interview your partner, he/she will interview you.

Partner's full name ______________________________

Age and date of birth ______________________________

Place of birth ______________________________

Family members ______________________________

Languages spoken ______________________________

Physical description: Hair color ____________________ Eye color ______________

Approximate height ______________

Grade ______________ Favorite subject ______________________________

Least favorite subject ______________________________

Involvement in sports, community activities, etc. ______________________________

____

Favorite movie ______________________________

Favorite TV show ______________________________

Favorite book ______________________________

Favorite magazine ______________________________

Favorite song or music group ______________________________

Favorite food ______________________________

What he/she hopes to do after high school . . . ______________________________

____

Name ______________________________ Date ____________________

175. Great Speech Openings

Have you ever had to deliver a speech? How did you open your speech? Some speeches open by telling a story or a joke. Others begin by putting questions to the audience. However your speech begins, it should be a powerful and memorable opening that will encourage people to listen to the rest of the speech. On this worksheet you will read the openings from some famous speeches. Read the openings and, in the spaces provided, indicate why the opening remarks are so strong and memorable. This exercise should help you the next time you deliver a speech.

> **"Five score years ago, a great American, in whose symbolic shadow we stand today, signed the Emancipation Proclamation. This momentous decree came as a great beacon light of hope to millions of Negro slaves who had been seared in the flames of withering injustice. It came as a joyous daybreak to end the long night of their captivity."**

Martin Luther King, Jr., "I Have a Dream"

Comments: ______________________________

____

____

> **"Fourscore and seven years ago our fathers brought forth on this continent a new nation, conceived in liberty, and dedicated to the proposition that all men are created equal. Now we are engaged in a great civil war, testing whether that nation, or any nation so conceived and so dedicated, can long endure. We are met on a great battlefield of that war. We have come to dedicate a portion of that field, as a final resting-place for those who here gave their lives that that nation might live. It is altogether fitting and proper that we should do this."**

Abraham Lincoln, "The Gettysburg Address"

Comments: ______________________________

____

____

> **"I stand before you today the representative of a family in grief, in a country in mourning before a world in shock. We are all united not only in our desire to pay respects to Diana but rather in our need to do so."**

Earl of Spencer's funeral oration for his sister, Princess Diana

Comments: ______________________________

____

____

176. First Letter/Last Letter

Teacher Instructions: This activity will teach your students to think on their feet. Arrange the class in a circle. Each person around the circle must give the name of a place or a famous person. The last letter of the name given must be the first letter of the next name. For example, if the first student says "Marilyn Monroe," then the second student must pick a person or place that begins with the letter "E." If that student says "Egypt," then the next student must come up with the name of a person or place that begins with "T" and so on.

Once your students are comfortable, you may want to adjust the game so that if the student cannot think of a name or place in two seconds (or the student picks a name or place that begins with the wrong letter), that player is out.

You may also want to increase the difficulty by only having students name a famous person and not a place as well.

This is a fun activity designed for the end of the week or as a warm-up before a public-speaking presentation. It is also a nonthreatening way to get the class speaking in front of their peers and thinking quickly.

Name ______________________ Date ______________

177. Evaluating Your Presentation and Public-Speaking Skills

This questionnaire is intended to help you evaluate your presentation and public-speaking skills. After each statement, circle the response that best applies to you. The questions for which you circle 2 or 3 indicate where you need to improve.

	ALWAYS	SOMETIMES	NEVER
1. For a formal speech or presentation, do you plan what you will say ahead of time?	1	2	3
2. Do you think of the needs of the audience before preparing and delivering your speech?	1	2	3
3. Do you develop an introduction that captures the interest of the audience (but still provides necessary information)?	1	2	3
4. Do your visual aids complement your presentation?	1	2	3
5. Do you maintain good eye contact with the audience?	1	2	3
6. Do you rehearse your speech before delivering it?	1	2	3
7. Is your voice strong, easy to hear, and not monotone?	1	2	3
8. Are your gestures natural and not distracting?	1	2	3
9. Do you express enthusiasm about the topic?	1	2	3
10. Do you avoid "reading" your notes word for word?	1	2	3

178. YOU BE THE JUDGE

TEACHER INSTRUCTIONS: Read the following legal case to the class and then follow the instructions printed below.

Jason and Donavon are two 17-year-old high school students who play on their school's basketball and volleyball teams. As well as being superb athletes, the two are also straight "A" students who plan on attending college on a full scholarship this fall.

One night while walking home from a party after drinking six bottles of beer, Jason and Donavon decided to steal a stop sign.

Later that night, the Wong family of six, driving home in a minivan from a camping trip, failed to stop at the intersection because there was no stop sign. The minivan hit a transport truck, and the entire Wong family was killed instantly.

Jason and Donavon have admitted to stealing the stop sign, which caused the six deaths. The Wongs' relatives want the boys convicted of murder. The boys are being tried as adults and, if found guilty, could face the death penalty.

Divide the class into three groups:

- Group One must argue that Jason and Donavon are guilty of murder.
- Group Two must argue that Jason and Donavon are NOT guilty of murder.
- Group Three is the jury. After listening to the evidence from both sides, the jury must determine whether the boys are guilty or not.

Name ______________________________ Date ________________

179. The Survival Game

Objective: This exercise is a fun way to try to convince other people to see things from your perspective. While you are trying to convince them to think a certain way, they are trying to convince you to see things from their perspective.

Instructions: It is the Fourth of July and the President has just announced that aliens have landed on Earth. You and your friends are escaping to a cabin. You have a fireplace and two beds in the cabin. The cabin is located near a fresh-water creek that flows into a lake 3 miles from the cabin. There is no electricity, running water, or food. You do not have time to gather many things to take with you. Below is a list of the things you might want. *You can only take 10 items.* Rank the items in order of priority. (#1 is the most important and #10 is the least important.)

Once you have chosen your items, get together with a small group and make a list of the 10 things you will take. Your group must agree on everything. Remember that everyone in your group will be staying at the cabin.

_____ a canoe
_____ a knife
_____ a box of matches
_____ a knapsack
_____ a quilt
_____ a map of the local area
_____ 40 feet of rope
_____ a bar of soap
_____ a pair of boots
_____ 4 candles
_____ 10 batteries
_____ 3 loaves of bread
_____ a bedsheet
_____ a raincoat
_____ a first-aid kit
_____ longjohns
_____ 1 package corn seeds and 1 package potato seeds
_____ a television set
_____ a 12 × 12 tarp
_____ a pillow
_____ a plate
_____ 20 teabags
_____ 4 tins of stew

_____ 2 paddles
_____ 1 lifejacket
_____ a pair of pants
_____ a gun with extra bullets
_____ a fishing rod with tackle
_____ a compass
_____ a radio (battery-operated)
_____ $300 in bills
_____ a Teddy bear
_____ a battery-operated lantern
_____ a carton of cigarettes
_____ 1 10-pound pail of granola
_____ 6 chocolate bars
_____ a wool sweater
_____ a credit card
_____ a cooking pot
_____ toilet paper
_____ a hairdryer
_____ a feather duvet
_____ a fork, knife, and spoon
_____ a mug
_____ 2 big jars of peanut butter
_____ a can opener

Note: You do not know how long you will be living in the wilderness. The only clothes you are wearing at the moment are a pair of jeans, socks, underwear, shoes, and a T-shirt.

Name ______________________________ Date ____________________

180. New World Adventure

Humans have just been given notice that Earth will explode next Tuesday. Not everyone can be saved. A spaceship has been hastily constructed with room for four people and plenty of supplies. The spaceship will land on Mars where its four passengers are expected to keep the human race alive.

You will be put in a group of 4–5. You are the members of a committee who have been selected to choose the four people who will represent the human race on Mars. Remember, these are the ONLY humans who will start the new world. Your group must agree unanimously on your choices.

1. Dr. Albert Letson—56 years old, male, black, astronaut, has never fathered any children
2. Dr. Jamie Carson—33 years old, female, white, astronaut, scientist, mother of 1
3. Doug Reid—17 years old, male, white, athletic high school student, never had children
4. Pierre Lapone—73 years old, white, male, former governor, father of 3, speaks 5 languages
5. Hung Mei—31 years old, male, Asian, construction worker, father of 2
6. Jessica Seminuik—22 years old, female, Native American, professional actress, never had children
7. Shahzad Ali—28 years old, male, East Indian, doctor, father of 1
8. Kim Arnold—30 years old, female, black, high school math & science teacher, mother of 1
9. Brooke Salt—18 years old, female, white, high school drop out, pregnant with twins
10. Sam Kent—40 years old, male, computer scientist, never had children
11. Giao Chow—22 years old, male, Asian, computer science university student, never had children
12. Kim Koo—1 year old, female, Asian, in perfect health
13. Fatima Atma—16 years old, female, East Indian, very athletic, honors student, gave up a baby for adoption last year
14. Carla Henderson—26 years old, female, white, lawyer, mother of twins

Your Four Choices:

____

____

Your Group's Choices:

____

____

181. AGREE/DISAGREE/UNDECIDED

TEACHER INSTRUCTIONS: The objective of this exercise is to encourage discussion, making it possible even for the quiet students to participate.

Set-Up

Post a sign in one corner of the room that states "Agree." On the diagonal corner of the room, post another sign that states "Disagree." On a corner of the room between the agree and disagree signs, post a third sign that states "Undecided."

How to Play

Read aloud one of the statements from the list below. The students must listen to the statement and then move to the corner with the sign that best describes their feelings. (For instance, if the student disagrees with the statement, then he or she must stand by the disagree sign.) The undecided sign is for students who are undecided about their feelings.

Once all the students have moved to the appropriate spot, you can encourage discussion by asking the students to give reasons for their position.

Suggestions

Inform the students that this activity is not intended to antagonize anyone but to stimulate discussion. It is important that students be open to opposing views.

Statements

(Please note that some of these statements may not be appropriate for all classes. You may also wish to create your own statements.)

1. Dogs make the best pets.
2. All Americans should learn to speak another language.
3. America needs a royal family like England has.
4. America needs a female president.
5. Professional athletes should be required to donate some of their earnings to charity.
6. All Americans should be required to learn how to use a computer.
7. Girls should be allowed to play on boys' sports teams.
8. People should get a parenting license before they can become parents.

182. The 30-Second Practice

Teacher Instructions: This exercise gives students an opportunity to become comfortable speaking in front of the class in a nonthreatening context.

Have the class sit in a circle. Read a question from the list to one student. Each student is given the next 30 seconds to answer the question. Proceed to the next student with the second question, etc.

1. Describe the ideal age to get married.
2. Where would you like to travel?
3. Why is junk food so popular?
4. What is your favorite movie?
5. What do you fear?
6. What is the greatest invention ever made?
7. If you could meet someone who has died, who would that person be?
8. What is your favorite season?
9. What is your favorite place in the world?
10. If you were eating your last meal, what would you choose to have?
11. If you could live anywhere in the world, where would you live?
12. What do you enjoy doing in your spare time?
13. What is the most ridiculous invention made by humans?
14. What types of people do you like to be around?
15. What type of music do you like?
16. Where is the last place in the United States that you would live?
17. If you only had $10 in the bank, what would you do with it?
18. If you could meet a celebrity, who would you like it to be?
19. If you could do whatever you wanted for one day, what would you do?
20. What do you think is the most important thing you have learned so far?
21. If you could go to the Olympics in any sport, which sport would you choose?
22. If you were given a million dollars, how would you spend it?
23. Who do you admire the most?
24. If you could be an animal, what animal would you most like to be?
25. What color best describes your personality?
26. What is the most important quality in a friend?
27. Who is the bravest person you know?
28. Who is the most important American of all time?
29. What was the worst period in world history?
30. If you could go back in time, where would you go?
31. What would be your ideal job?
32. What is your favorite possession?
33. What was your favorite book as a child?
34. What do you like to do on a rainy day?
35. What do you hope people say about you in 50 years?

Name ______________________ Date ______________

183. Time Capsule

Imagine it is the year 2312. A lone spaceship from another galaxy has just landed on Earth. Since the nuclear war of 2072, our planet has been uninhabited. However, years before the nuclear war, a group of American students created a time capsule to show future generations what life was like in America in the early 21st century.

You are part of that group of American students and your mission is to choose 10 items for the time capsule. Choose the 10 items and then explain WHY you have chosen each item.

184. Modified Telephone

Teacher Instructions: Give the person at the end of each row a slip of paper with a message on it. Have the person read the message silently and then whisper it into the ear of the person in front of him or her. It is important that the student does not show the message to anyone else. Then the second person whispers the message into the ear of the third person and so on until the message has been delivered to the first person in the row. At this point, the first person in the row writes the message on the board. When all the groups are finished, the person at the end of each row should read his or her message to the class. The class can then determine whether the message on the board remotely resembles the original.

This activity works well if your class is sitting in rows. If they are in another seating formation, you may need to modify the activity slightly.

Each row should have a different message.

MESSAGE 1: Tammy's truck got towed to Toledo on Tuesday.

MESSAGE 2: Susie sits on Sunday afternoons and sips soda.

MESSAGE 3: Carl craves catfish with ketchup on a Kaiser bun.

MESSAGE 4: Peter picks pickles to make pickled preserves.

MESSAGE 5: Five friends fried French fries for Fanny.

MESSAGE 6: Libby likes liverwurst, while Lena likes Leonard.

MESSAGE 7: William wrote weekend weather reports in the Washington Times.

MESSAGE 8: Earl eats eggs daily except at Easter.

MESSAGE 9: Melanie makes marvelous melon muffins on Mondays.

MESSAGE 10: Synchronized swimmers sink in swampy pools.

MESSAGE 11: Greta grows green grapes in Greenland.

MESSAGE 12: Wendy wants warm weather on Wednesday.

185. How Many Uses for an Object?

Teacher Instructions: Give the class one of the items from the list below. (If you do not have the item, tell them what it is. However, this activity works better if you have the actual item.) Ask each student to suggest an application of this object that has nothing to do with its intended use. For example, a student could suggest that the banana be used as a telephone or a hairbrush. The students, however, must come up with a use that has not been already mentioned.

This exercise allows students to think on their feet!

A Banana

A Button

A Newspaper

A Hammer

A Pencil

A Skipping Rope

A Ruler

186. COMMUNICATION EXERCISE

TEACHER INSTRUCTIONS: The objective of this exercise is to improve listening skills, while also teaching students the importance of two-way communication and the clarification given by, for example, hand gestures.

One student is given the following diagram. Do NOT show the diagram to the group. The student must describe the diagram to the group, while each person in the group tries to duplicate it on a piece of paper. The group may not ask questions and the student who is describing the diagram may not use hand gestures.

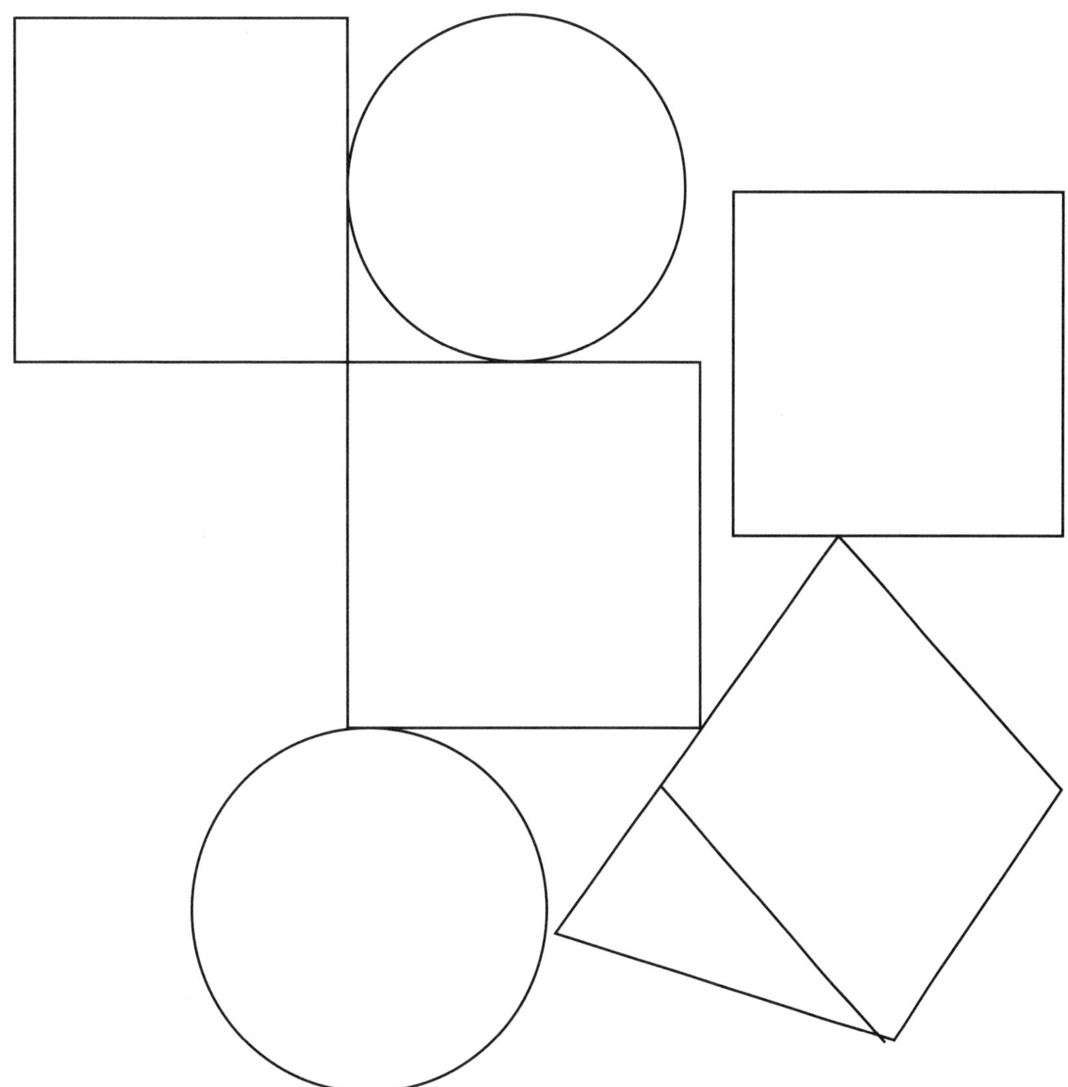

187. CHARADES

TEACHER INSTRUCTIONS: Actions can speak louder than words, as the following activity demonstrates. The game is Charades. Class members take turns in front of the class. A person, place, or thing is whispered to the student who acts out the secret word without speaking. The class needs to guess what the person, place, or thing is. You may wish to help students by specifying the category.

Here is a list of things the class can act out. You may wish to add to this list.

Person: Elvis Presley

Place: Australia

Thing: A bookshelf

Person: Muhammad Ali

Place: The White House

Thing: TV dinner

Person: Abraham Lincoln

Place: The Grand Canyon

Thing: Drive-in movie theater

Name ________________________________ Date ____________________

188. Listening Skills Quiz

This quiz will teach you how to improve your listening skills. Write *true* if the statement is true and *false* if the statement is false.

__________ 1. Good listeners plan what they are going to say next instead of focusing on what the speaker is saying.

__________ 2. Good listeners never interrupt in order to add their opinion until the speaker is done talking.

__________ 3. Good listeners focus on what is being said and how it is being said. They recognize that nonverbal cues sometimes speak louder than words.

__________ 4. Good listeners never make eye contact with the speaker.

__________ 5. Good listeners are open-minded and never critical or judgmental of what the speaker is saying.

__________ 6. Good listeners occasionally interject into the conversation phrases such as "I see" or "That's interesting" in order to show the speaker that the listener is paying attention.

__________ 7. Good listeners try to avoid distorting the information they hear.

__________ 8. Good listeners know that the speaker is more important in a conversation than the listener.

__________ 9. Good listeners do not get distracted by things going on around them.

__________ 10. Good listeners ask intelligent questions about what the speaker has been saying.

__________ 11. Good listeners know that it is impossible to listen and speak at the same time.

__________ 12. Good listeners realize that listening is a skill that can be improved with a conscious effort.

189. The Substitute Teacher's Day

Teacher Instructions: Pass out copies of the "Substitute Teacher's Day" seating plan. Then read this script aloud as the class writes the students' names in the appropriate places on the seating plan. Do NOT repeat any parts of this script as you are reading it.

The Script:

When Miss Appleby arrived at Meadowvale High School for a day of substitute teaching, she was relieved when she got the class list for the tenth-grade English class in first period as there were only ten students in the class.

"Ten students!" Miss Appleby thought to herself. "This is going to be a piece of cake."

However, Miss Appleby was in for a surprise. When the bell rang, there were only nine students in the room. As the National Anthem ended, Jerry Bond, who had a black eye, stumbled into the room and sat at his desk next to the window.

"Why are you late, Jerry?" Miss Appleby asked.

Jerry could not answer because he was trying to stop the blood that was gushing out of his nose from getting all over his books.

"Jerry, I think you should go to the nurse's office. Will anyone help Jerry? I don't think he should go alone," said Miss Appleby.

Ashley Anderson, who sits in the first seat in Jerry's row, was chosen to go.

"Why did you pick Ashley?" asked Kevin Taylor who sat next to Ashley. "She always gets to do stuff like that."

As Kevin complained, his friend next to him, Joel Ford, threw a paper airplane across the room. While Miss Appleby dealt with Joel, Caroline Carson, who sat by the pencil sharpener, started sharpening her pencil, while the identical twins, Rory and Cory MacKenzie, started to fight. Miss Appleby could not tell the twins apart, but she knew from her seating plan that Rory sat next to Caroline and Cory sat beside Jerry. Meanwhile, Adam Walker, who sat by the door, wandered over to the window, opened it, and started yelling to his buddies outside.

Just as Miss Appleby was about to lose control, Mary Little screamed from her desk in the back corner, "BE QUIET!"

Everyone settled down for three minutes and then, fortunately, the bell rang. As Miss Appleby gathered her books, Carrie Sloan, Cory's neighbor, said, "I hope your next class is better."

Miss Appleby hoped so too.

Name ______________________________ Date ____________________

189A. The Substitute Teacher's Day

Your teacher will read you a short tale about a substitute teacher's day at Meadowvale High School. As the story is read, listen carefully and write the name of each student in the correct place.

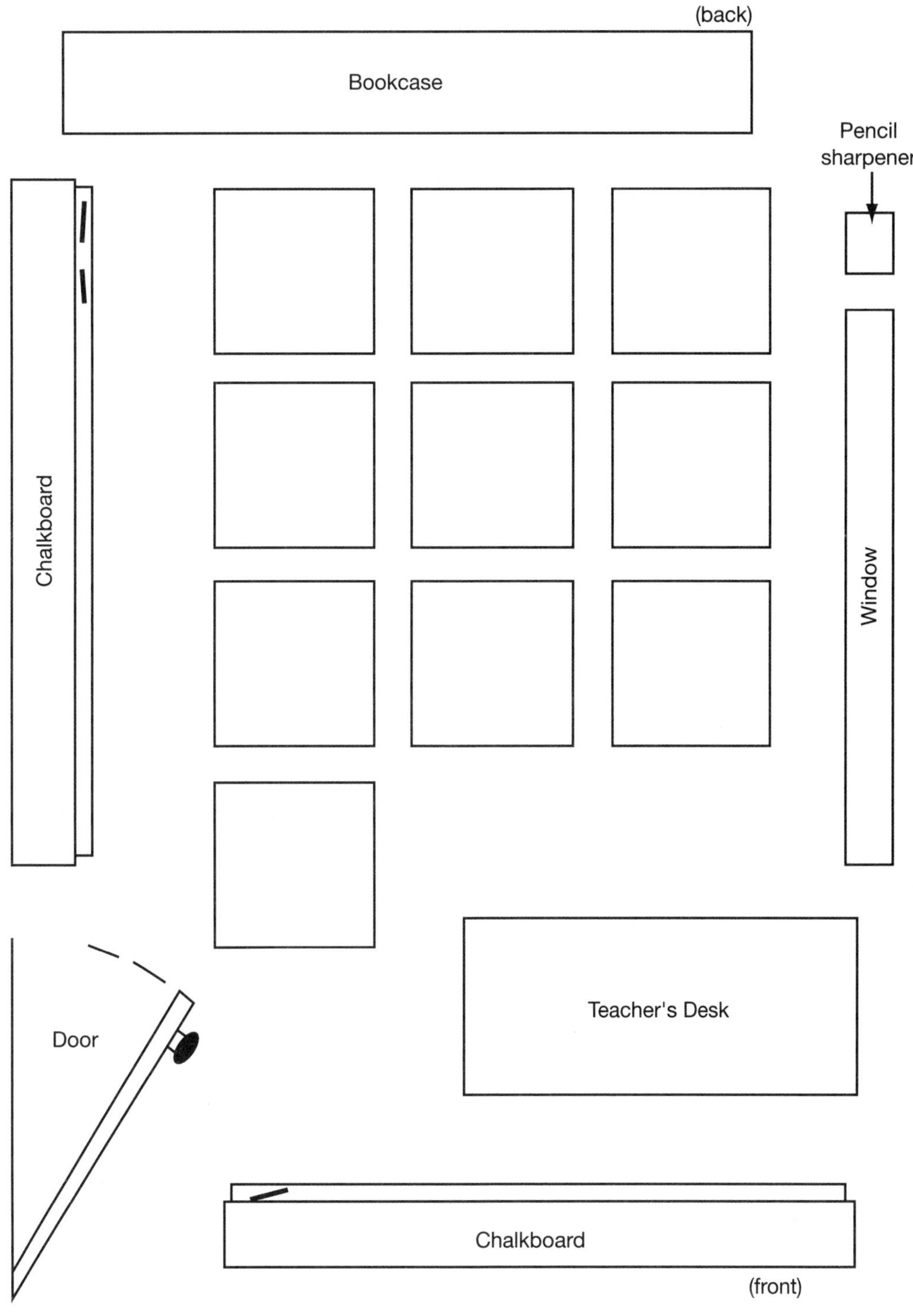

190. The Shopping Trip

Teacher Instructions: Give each student a copy of the sheet called "The Shopping Trip." Read the following script aloud to the students. Do NOT repeat any sections of the script.

The Script:

Laura, who happened to be an identical triplet, was meeting one of her sisters downtown for a shopping trip. Layla and Lisa were the other two triplets, but Laura only planned to shop with Layla.

Laura arrived 20 minutes early, so she walked up the steps from the subway and headed directly across the street to Coffee Time. There, Laura waited at a seat by the window, while sipping her coffee. Laura could not wait to start shopping because there was a big sale at Holt Renfrew, which was the big department store at the corner of Manitoba and Montgomery. She also planned to shop at The Bombay Company, which was at the other corner of Manitoba and Montgomery, and The Jean Machine, which was located next to the news stand.

While sipping her coffee, Laura looked across the street and saw Layla walk into a restaurant called The Daily Grill, which was next to the subway stairs.

"Oh no," thought Laura. "Layla must have forgotten where we planned to meet." Then she watched Layla leave the restaurant and head next door to McDonald's. "I better go and meet her before she heads to McDonalds' neighbor, Payless Shoes," Laura muttered to herself.

Before Laura could walk across the street, Layla left the restaurant and headed across the street to Hall's Drugstore, which was located next to Coffee Time. As soon as Layla walked across the street, Laura greeted her and laughed because it was not Layla; it was *Lisa* who was on her own excursion to the sale at Fairweather, situated next to The Jean Machine.

Laura told Lisa about her plan to meet Layla. Lisa decided to join them and when Layla arrived, the three sisters began their shopping spree at The Body Shop on Montgomery Lane.

Name ______________________________ Date ____________________

190A. The Shopping Trip

Your teacher will read you a short tale about a shopping trip. As the story is being read, listen carefully and write the name of each shop in the correct place on the plan.

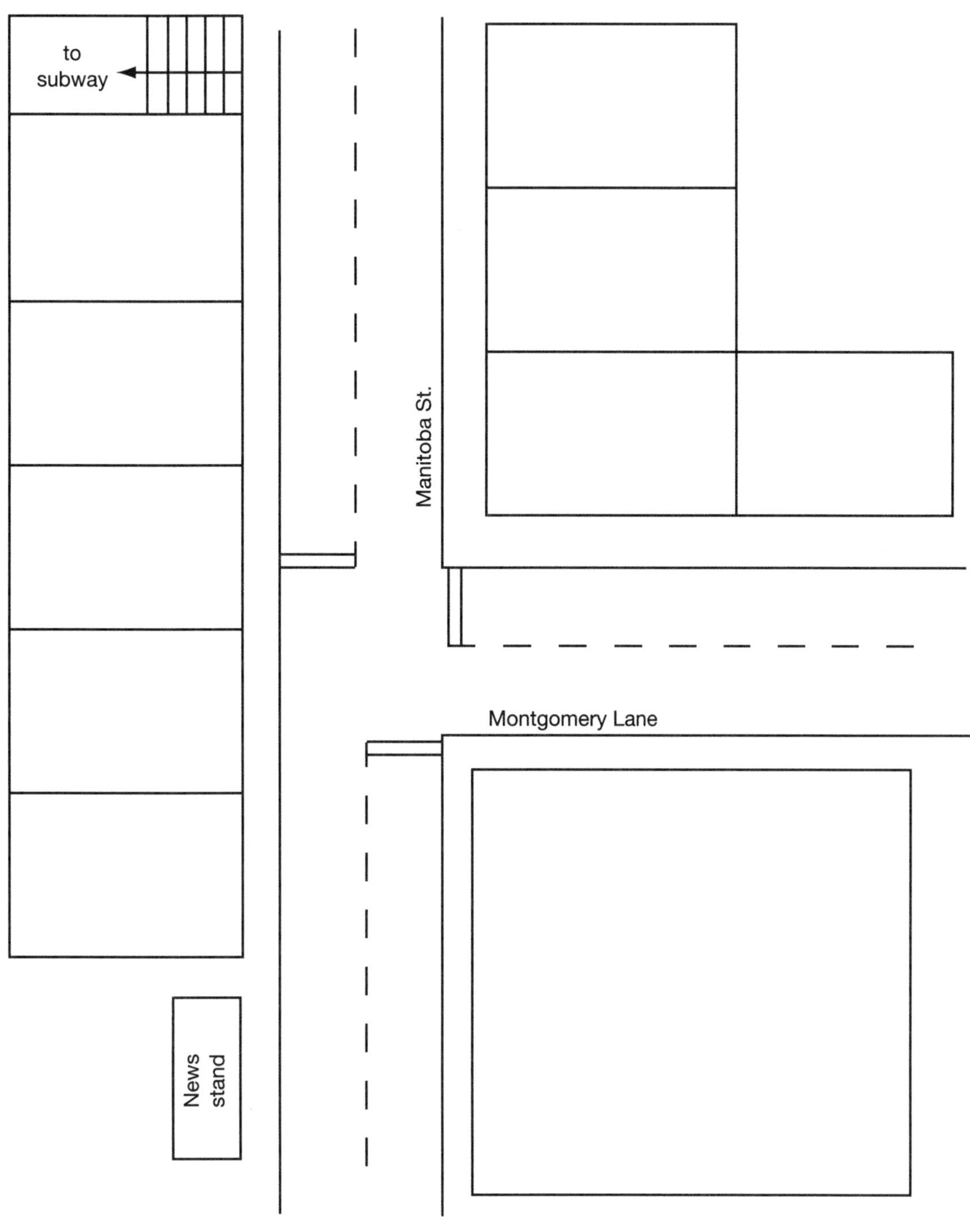

191. The Listening Grid

Teacher Instructions: Read these instructions aloud to the students. While you are reading these instructions, the students will be blackening the appropriate box from the grid. Do not repeat any of the instructions.

Across	Down
9	3
12	8
10	14
16	16
7	9
7	11
14	11
6	15
15	15
20	17
12	6
9	11
11	13
13	14
19	17
5	11
10	2
12	11
18	16
8	6
9	13
1	17
11	5
17	16
8	14
2	17

Across	Down
12	4
14	14
8	8
15	11
8	11
8	4
12	14
14	10
4	16
11	3
10	11
13	9
11	11
5	16
6	10
9	5
13	11
11	14
9	12
7	14
13	7
11	12
9	14
6	11
7	7

Name ______________________________ Date ____________________

191A. The Listening Grid

This listening exercise tests your ability to follow verbal instructions. Listen to your teacher and move where your teacher tells you on the grid. For example, the blackened box below is located 3 boxes from the left and 16 boxes down. This would be described by your teacher as "3 across and 16 down." Color in the box after each instruction is given. Your teacher will not repeat instructions, so you may wish to put an X in each box and shade it in later.

When you've finished, you will have drawn a ______________________________.

	1	2	3	4	5	6	7	8	9	10	11	12	13	14	15	16	17	18	19	20
1																				
2																				
3																				
4																				
5																				
6																				
7																				
8																				
9																				
10																				
11																				
12																				
13																				
14																				
15																				
16																				
17																				

Name ______________________________ Date ________________

192. What's Missing?

Teacher Instructions: Read the following to the class.

"I will read a poem to you. Listen carefully. After reading the poem, I will give you a copy of the poem with some of the words missing. You will need to fill in the missing words."

The Poem

(read by the teacher)

In my dream last night
Nothing real was right.
A snake baked.
A pig jigged.
A llama who was cocky
  began to play ice hockey.
On a beach, tanning, was a polar bear.
In a race, the tortoise lost to the hare.
My brother became a rat
  chased by the neighbor's cat.
My father was a lion
  eating my brother Ryan.
Mom barked like a dog,
  but looked like a hog.
So tonight I cannot close my eyes.
I fear what dreams will materialize.

Name ______________________________ Date ____________________

192A. What's Missing?

This activity tests your listening skills. Which words go in the blank spaces?

In my ________________________ last night

Nothing real was ________________________.

A snake baked.

A pig ________________________.

A ________________________ who was cocky

began to play ice hockey.

On a ________________________, tanning, was a polar bear.

In a race, the tortoise lost to the ________________________.

My ________________________ became a rat

chased by the ________________________ cat.

My ________________________ was a lion

eating my brother Ryan.

Mom ________________________ like a dog,

but looked like a hog.

So ________________________ I cannot close my eyes.

I fear what ________________________ will materialize.

Name ______________________________ Date ____________________

193. A Listening Poem

Teacher Instructions: Read the poem "A Day at the Office" aloud two times and then have the class answer the questions on the worksheet. *Pass out the worksheet after the second reading.*

A Day at the Office

A full house
Of which the musicians seem
Calmly unaware.

They arrive,
  Swinging a flute case
  Or burdened by the bulk of a double bass.

And as always
  The principal cellist arrives five minutes before the show,
  Looking almost bored.
  (He's done it so many times before.)

A few of them
  Play parts from the pieces.

Others tune.

Some do scales.

Two of the violinists gossip about the tuba player's drinking habits,
The clarinetist's attractive wife's awful cooking,
And the difficulty in toilet training a two-year-old.

A bald violinist cushions his instrument with his extra chins.

The principal violinist takes his place.

The conductor marches to the podium.

The audience hushes.

The musicians raise their eyes
And their instruments.
The conductor raises his arms . . .

A day at the office has begun.

—Sandra McTavish

Name ______________________________ Date ____________________

193A. A Listening Poem

How well do you listen? After listening to the poem that has been read twice by your teacher, answer the following questions:

1. What is the name of the poem?

   ____

2. Who arrives five minutes before the show?

   ____

3. What does the conductor raise?

   ____

4. What three things do the two violinists talk about?

   ____

   ____

   ____

5. How does the bald violinist cushion his instrument?

   ____

6. How many people are in the audience?

   ____

7. List all the instruments mentioned in the poem.

   ____

   ____

   ____

Section 8

WORD FUN

"The real character of a man is found out by his amusements."

Sir Joshua Reynolds

Name ______________________________ Date ____________________

194. Which Letter Comes Next?

Examine the pattern of letters and try to determine which letter should come next. Write that letter in the blank space at the end of the pattern.

For example: B D F H J

1. Z Y X W V U ____
2. F H K O ____
3. Q O M K I G ____
4. U O I E ____
5. H I G J F ____
6. B Y C X D W E ____
7. E J O T ____
8. D N I S N ____
9. G H I J K L M N ____
10. B D F H J L ____

Name ______________________ Date ______________

195. Simon Says

Do what Simon tells you to do.

Simon Says . . .
Take an 8-letter word
for drink that starts with "B." ______________

Simon Says . . .
Drop the first four letters. ______________

Simon Says . . .
Change the first letter to a "P." ______________

Simon Says . . .
Add an "L" after the first letter
and change the "G" to a "T." ______________

Simon Says . . .
Drop the first letter. ______________

Simon Says . . .
Add an "R" at the end of the word. ______________

Simon Says . . .
Add a "T" before the "T." ______________

Simon Says . . .
Change the "L" to a "B." ______________

Simon Says . . .
Drop the last three letters. ______________

Simon Says . . .
Change the "B" to a "C." ______________

Simon Says . . .
Add "egory" to the end of the word.
What do you have? ______________

Name ______________________________________ Date ____________________

196. A Simile Snake

A simile is a figure of speech that uses the words *like* or *as* to compare two unlike things. For example, *the old lady waddles like a duck* is a simile. Fill in the blanks to complete the simile and then write the word in the appropriate spot in the crossword. The last letter of each word is the first letter of the next word.

1. He ran around like a chicken with its head ____________ off.
2. The senior citizen stood out like a sore ____________ at the high school party.
3. She sings so well that she sings like a ____________.
4. Alice and Tung fought like a cat and ____________.
5. That towel is as green as ____________.
6. The cement walk is as rough as ____________.
7. That famous model is as skinny as a ____________.
8. The newborn baby is as meek as a ____________.
9. Before the garage sale, her mother was as busy as a ____________.
10. Everybody was quiet in the woods except Lucy who walked like an ____________.
11. "Are you sure Kim's older?" "I'm as certain as death and ____________."
12. Raj's five-year-old brother is so wild that he's like a bull in a china ____________.
13. If you enter Dave's room, watch out! He's as messy as a ____________.
14. Those jeans are so tight that they fit like a ____________.
15. He wished he could grow wings and fly like an ____________.
16. I don't trust Jody; he's as slippery as an ____________.
17. He slept like a ____________, which shows how tired he was.

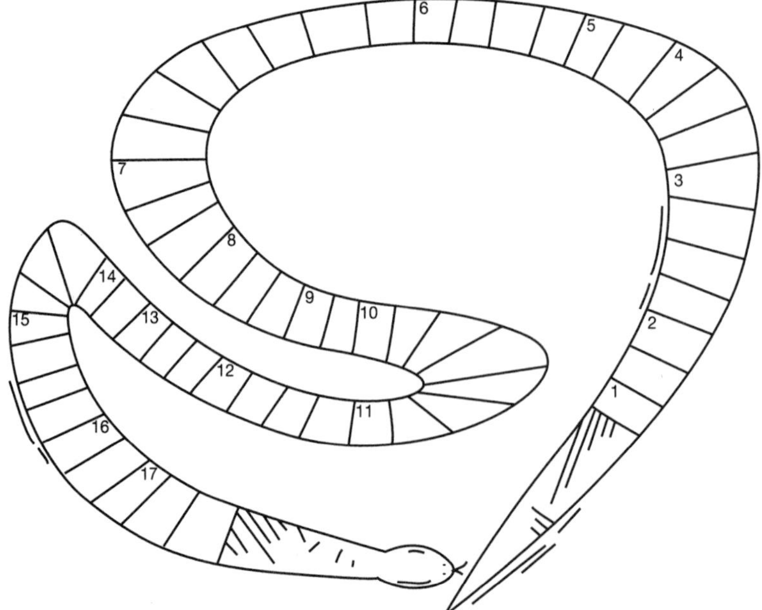

Name ______________________________ Date ____________________

197. A Palindrome Letter

Palindromes are words that are spelled the same forward and backward. For example, the words *nun* and *level* are palindromes. Read the following letter from Otto and fill in the blanks with the appropriate palindromes.

Dear ____________________ (mother) ***and*** ____________________ (father)***,***

How are you? ____________________ (exclamation)***!! Camp is fun!*** ____________________ (past tense of "do") ***you get my last letter? I wrote it yesterday. Don't worry, I'm starting to get over my homesickness. I realize it is the*** ____________________ (night and early evening) ***of my last day, but I'm going to try not to seem too excited about leaving at*** ____________________ (middle of the day) ***tomorrow. Yesterday I went in a*** ____________________ (a type of canoe) ***and tipped. Then I wanted to buy a*** ____________________ (soda) ***at the snack shop, but I have no money left because I've spent it all on stamps. Last night a guy named*** ____________________ (Robert) ***in my cabin played a*** ____________________ (trick) ***on me. He put my hand in warm water while I slept. I don't need to tell you what happened. After noticing my wet sleeping bag, I was teased and called a*** ____________________ (young child)***.*** ____________________ (Robert) ***and I got into a fight after the incident and now I am the proud owner of a black*** ____________________ (organ of vision)***. Say hi to*** ____________________ (female sibling) ***for me. I can't believe I actually miss her.***

See you tomorrow!

Love, ____________________ (male name, sounds like auto)

Name ______________________________ Date ____________________

198. Word Chains

Connect the words in each word chain by adding letters in the spaces to create a word. The last letter of the given word will be the first letter of the word in the link, and the last letter of the word in the link will be the first letter of the next word that is given. The link words that you provide must be actual words.

Here is an example:

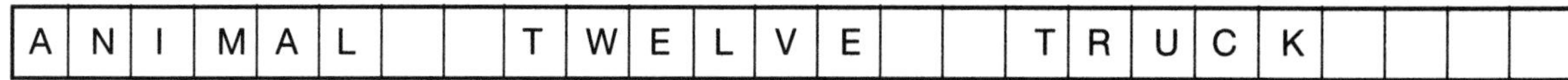

If you add

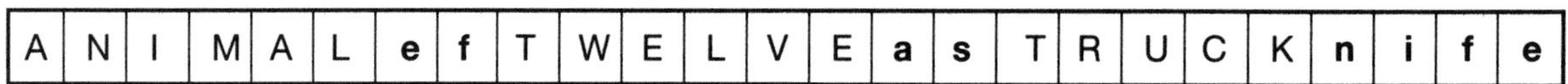

the new words in the link will be **LEFT, EAST,** and **KNIFE.**

Now it is your turn:

Chain 1

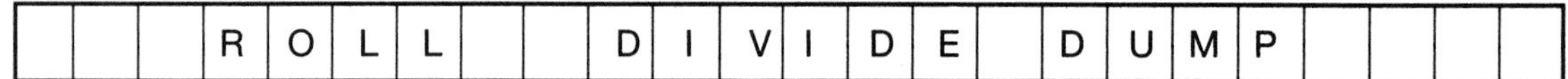

Chain 2

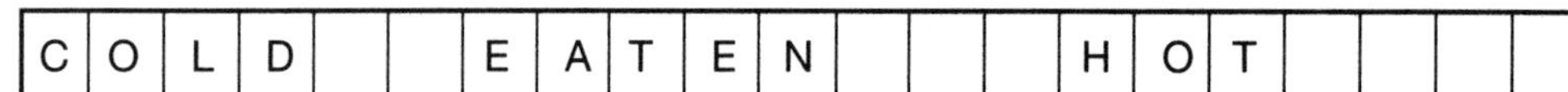

Chain 3

Chain 4

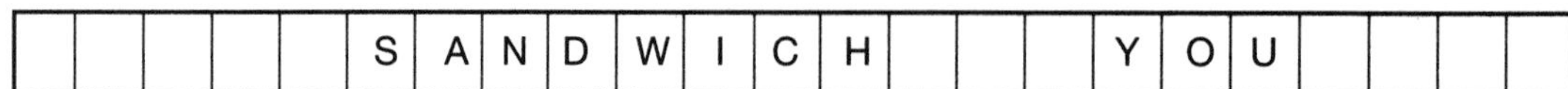

Chain 5

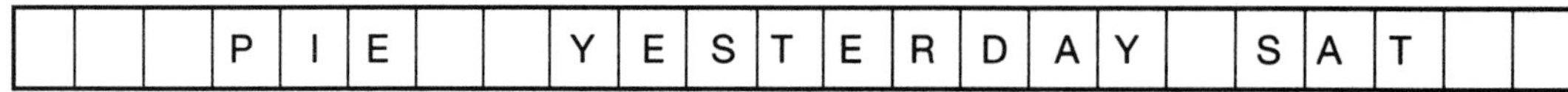

Name ______________________ Date ______________

199. It Takes Three

The words grouped below may appear to be unrelated. However, all the words belong in clusters of three beside the clues. Some words may fit in more than one cluster, so you may need to do some rearranging to make sure all the words fit.

Airplane	Canada	Georgia	Mountains	South Carolina
Alaska	Cliffs	Hawaii	New York	Star
Alexandra	Clinton	Hills	Nile	Toyota
Amazon	Dallas	Honda	Pluto	Venus
Bird	Denver	Lincoln	Russia	Virginia
Boston	Ford	Mississippi	Saturn	Washington

1. States ______________________
2. Car companies ______________________
3. First names ______________________
4. Planets ______________________
5. Rivers ______________________
6. High ground ______________________
7. Places in the North ______________________
8. In the sky ______________________
9. Presidents ______________________
10. Cities ______________________

Name ______________________________ Date ____________________

200. Career Alphabet

Think of a career that begins with each letter of the alphabet.

A ____________________

B ____________________

C ____________________

D ____________________

E ____________________

F ____________________

G ____________________

H ____________________

I ____________________

J ____________________

K ____________________

L ____________________

M ____________________

N ____________________

O ____________________

P ____________________

Q ____________________

R ____________________

S ____________________

T ____________________

U ____________________

V ____________________

W ____________________

X ____________________

Y ____________________

Z ____________________

Name ________________________________ Date ____________________

201. Word Removal

Follow the instructions and cross out the appropriate words in the chart at the bottom of the page. When you are finished, you will have a message that reads from left to right. Some words may be eliminated by more than one instruction.

The message reads: ____

1. In columns 1 and 3, cross out every word that ends in "e."
2. Cross out all words that begin with the letter "s."
3. Cross out all three-letter words.
4. Cross out all words that relate to water.
5. In columns 3 and 4, cross out all words that begin with the first 8 letters of the alphabet.
6. Cross out all words that are cities or states.
7. Cross out all words that are homonyms.

(1)	(2)	(3)	(4)
hike	sentence	but	sure
the	Denver	Europe	cargo
treat	ocean	eliminate	tie
rain	and	with	South Carolina
see	shoes	driveway	Rhode Island
Kansas City	your	student	respect
since	everyone	hyper	balloon
one	Detroit	puddle	old
break	suffer	ache	their
minute	put	grass	should

Name ______________________________ Date ____________________

202. ANALOGIES

Analogies are pairs of words with relationships. The first pair of words determines the relationship of the second pair of words. For example:

UP is to DOWN as IN is to ____OUT____

(UP is the opposite of DOWN; therefore, the proper analogy for IN is its opposite: OUT.) Fill in the blank with the analogous word based on the relationship established by the first pair of words.

1. WEST is to EAST as LEFT is to ____________________
2. PEOPLE is to HOME as BIRD is to ____________________
3. TWO is to FOUR as FIVE is to ____________________
4. MONDAY is to TUESDAY as MAY is to ____________________
5. COW is to HERD as WOLF is to ____________________
6. BATHING SUIT is to SWIMMER as HELMET is to ____________________
7. DRIVE is to CAR as ____________________ is to BIKE
8. JUDGE is to COURTROOM as ____________________ is to SCHOOL
9. A is to C as ONE is to ____________________
10. GRASS is to GREEN as SUN is to ____________________
11. SPRING is to SUMMER as ____________________ is to AFTERNOON
12. DANCE is to DANCER as ____________________ is to DIVER
13. STOP is to START as WIN is to ____________________
14. D is to FOUR as G is to ____________________
15. COW is to ANIMAL as MOSQUITO is to ____________________
16. ELEMENTARY SCHOOL is to HIGH SCHOOL as CHILD is to ____________________
17. UP is to NORTH as DOWN is to ____________________
18. CARROT is to ORANGE as LETTUCE is to ____________________

Name ______________________________ Date ____________________

203. School Scramble

Each scrambled word, unscrambled, relates in some way to school. Unscramble each word if you can.

1. RHEYPGAOG ____________________
2. DTTESUN ____________________
3. KCALH ____________________
4. ASLTA ____________________
5. SOSORLCAM ____________________
6. PNLAICIRP ____________________
7. DIRENB ____________________
8. AEMXNTNIIAO ____________________
9. OTXKTBEO ____________________
10. TEAFEACRI ____________________
11. CNPIEL ____________________
12. SHAITTMMAEC ____________________

Name ______________________ Date ______________

204. Word Building

How many smaller words can you get from:

United States

George Washington

Name ______________________________ Date ____________________

205. Alphabet Soup

There are 26 empty boxes in the middle of the chart. Insert a different letter of the alphabet into each box to form a word of five or more letters reading across. The letter you add may be from the beginning, middle, or end of the word. *All the letters in the row may not necessarily be part of the word.*

A B C D E F G H I J K L M N O P Q R S T U V W X Y Z

L	O	T	O	G		T	H	E	R	S
G	F	R	I	E		D	S	H	I	P
D	I	F	F	I		E	D	R	O	K
T	U	B	A	N		N	A	O	R	A
T	R	E	M	E		B	E	R	T	E
W	V	E	G	E		A	B	L	E	S
O	H	O	R	R		B	L	E	L	T
F	R	I	T	E		E	F	O	R	E
F	A	T	H	E		H	V	Q	U	B
M	D	A	M	A		E	P	K	H	R
C	I	C	R	A		Y	E	A	N	E
K	A	D	F	I		T	I	O	N	S
F	I	N	I	S		S	T	A	R	M
N	O	T	A	L		A	M	O	U	S
B	R	V	E	L		U	I	E	T	Y
K	A	B	R	A		E	S	L	O	P
S	H	A	P	P		E	R	M	I	T
L	S	T	E	A		N	I	G	B	O
M	O	B	V	I		U	S	A	W	M
M	A	R	V	E		O	U	S	A	T
U	N	P	R	E		A	R	E	D	U
C	E	S	E	N		A	T	I	O	N
R	I	C	O	B		E	A	L	T	H
A	B	C	F	K		O	L	L	Y	D
W	O	S	T	U		E	N	T	A	P
R	O	A	M	B		L	A	N	C	E

Name ______________________________ Date ____________________

206. Word Changes

Go from the word *TALK* to *SOLD* by changing one letter at a time. Each time you change a letter, it must be a word.

TALK

____

____

____

SOLD

Go from the word *DOVE* to *LIFT* by changing one letter at a time. Each time you change a letter, it must be a word.

DOVE

____

____

____

LIFT

Name ______________________ Date ______________

207. Unsolved Mysteries

A coded note has been left for the trainees at the Maryland State Police Academy. The trainees are unable to solve this. Can you do it?

Here is your only clue: A = Z

RU BLF HLOEV

GSRH NBHGVIB

BLF NZB DZMG

GL XLMHRWVI

Z XZIVVI

ZH Z KIREZGV

RMEVHGRTZGLI

Name ______________________________ Date ____________________

208. Rhyming Pairs

Read the clues on the left-hand side to determine the rhyming pairs. Write the two words that rhyme (matching the clue) on the lines. For example:

A happy father ___glad___ ___dad___

1. Twins who are bad ____________ ____________
2. A box made out of metal ____________ ____________
3. Highest-ranking police officer ____________ ____________
4. A store for brooms ____________ ____________
5. An enemy named Joseph ____________ ____________
6. A polluted mist ____________ ____________
7. A romance after winter ____________ ____________
8. Rich metal was purchased ____________ ____________
9. When you don't cry ____________ ____________
10. A dance in autumn ____________ ____________
11. A sad circus guy ____________ ____________
12. Emotional on her wedding day ____________ ____________

Name ______________________________ Date ________________

209. What Is the Mystery Word?

Using the information in the chart as a guide, and working downwards, determine what is the mystery word.

PART OF SPEECH	**NOUN**	**NOUN**	**VERB**	**NOUN**	**VERB**
STARTS WITH THE LETTER . . .	S	C	L	A	B
ENDS WITH THE LETTER . . .	E	S	K	E	H
NUMBER OF LETTERS	7	9	4	5	5
CLUE	*a subject in school*	*a festive period*	*using sight*	*a fruit*	*happens when you get embarrassed*
WHAT IS THE WORD?					

Name ______________________________ Date ____________________

210. Letter Math

Complete each six-letter word by identifying the missing letters. Each letter of the alphabet has been given a numerical value (see the box below). Determine which letters are missing that would complete the sum of the word.

For example, ANIMAL would be A _____ I M _____ L = 50
1 + 14 + 9 + 13 + 1 + 12 = 50

A = 1	B = 2	C = 3	D = 4	E = 5	F = 6	G = 7	H = 8	I = 9	J = 10
K = 11	L = 12	M = 13	N = 14	O = 15	P = 16	Q = 17	R = 18	S = 19	T = 20
		U = 21	V = 22	W = 23	X = 24	Y = 25	Z = 26		

1. M ____ T ____ E R = 79
2. ____ E I ____ H ____ = 57
3. N ____ B O ____ Y = 75
4. C ____ F ____ E ____ = 40
5. ____ O N ____ E ____ = 83
6. E N ____ I ____ E = 54
7. L ____ M ____ E ____ = 71
8. O ____ A N ____ E = 60
9. ____ O L L ____ R = 62
10. S T ____ ____ ____ G = 93
11. D ____ I V ____ R = 76
12. B ____ T ____ O ____ = 85

Name ______________________________ Date ____________________

211. Another Word Removal

Follow the instructions and cross out the appropriate words in the chart. When you are finished, you will have a message that reads from left to right. Some of the words may be eliminated by more than one instruction.

The message reads: ____

1. In columns 1 and 4, cross out all four-letter words.
2. In column 2, cross out all two-letter words.
3. In columns 2, 3, and 4, cross out all words that end with the letter "e."
4. Cross out all words that rhyme with "bump."
5. Cross out any words that are things that can be found in a physical education class.
6. In columns 1 and 4, cross out all words that are homophones.
7. Cross out any contractions.
8. In columns 2 and 3, cross out any words that are 7 letters or more.

(1)	(2)	(3)	(4)
Jump	Didn't	Stump	Pedal
I'll	It	Triumphant	Sing
Eat	Racket	State	Too
I	Free	Ball	Pie
Trump	Another	Dump	Obey
Net	Lots	Name	Football
Side	So	Librarian	Play
Let's	Classmate	Of	Grump
Over	Ate	Separate	Soft
Rule	Be	You've	Vegetables

Name ______________________________ Date ____________________

212. Going on a Camping Trip

You are going on a camping trip with your friends.

You can take an apple,
but you cannot take an orange.

You can take a kitten,
but you cannot take a cat.

You can take a baseball,
but you cannot take a bat.

After looking very closely at what you can take, and considering the differences between those items and the things you cannot take, list 10 items that you *can* take.

1. ______________________________
2. ______________________________
3. ______________________________
4. ______________________________
5. ______________________________
6. ______________________________
7. ______________________________
8. ______________________________
9. ______________________________
10. ______________________________

Name ______________________________ Date ______________

213. What's the Word?

Each box contains a clue for a familiar word or phrase. For example, the answer to A-1 is coffee break. Can you solve the other 24?

	A	B	C	D	E
1	cof fee	school	C H A I R	Dance Dance Dance Dance	T O W N
2	oholene	ground feet feet feet feet feet feet	TIME	**TEA 4 TEA**	blesdou
3			**BOOK** ✔	**HAR MO NY**	pLOT
4	**SLEEPING JOB**	r r a a i i l w w a a y y		moodmoodmood	CREEK PADDLE
5	TROUBLE TROUBLE	I **TO IT** GET WILL	CAR GARAGE CAR	**DRUG** **DOSE**	out

Name ______________________ Date ______________

214. Letter Pairs

Listed below are ten 10-letter words. The words are divided into letter pairs. Each word is missing at least one pair of letters from the letter pile. Put the appropriate letter pairs in each word to complete the word. You will only use each letter pair once.

1.	AM		LA		ES
2.	PR		AG		DA
3.		ND		LA	ND
4.	CH		SE		KE
5.	SA	LU		TI	ON
6.		US	EW		ES
7.	WO		PE		ER
8.		CT	IO		RY
9.	RE		IR		OR
10.	TR		MP		NT

Letter pile:

AT, NA, BU, CK, ER, HA, WO, SP, IU, DI, AN, EE, OD, OP, TA, CA, IV, NC, HO

Name ______________________________ Date ______________

215. More Alphabet Soup

There are 26 empty boxes in the middle of the chart. Insert a different letter of the alphabet into each box to form a word of five or more letters reading across. The letter you add may come from the beginning, middle, or end of the word. *All the letters in the row may not necessarily be part of the word.*

A B C D E F G H I J K L M N O P Q R S T U V W X Y Z

W	H	A	D	B		O	T	H	E	R
O	V	E	A	R		I	C	L	E	S
I	N	T	R	O		U	C	E	G	G
C	A	R	D	E		A	M	P	U	S
V	E	R	S	I		N	O	P	E	R
D	E	S	I	G		P	E	O	P	E
S	I	D	P	C		N	T	U	R	Y
S	T	F	L	E		I	B	L	E	R
K	O	B	U	S		N	E	S	S	E
E	X	T	R	O		S	I	N	G	T
C	A	L	A	P		R	O	A	C	H
F	R	A	N	T		R	O	N	G	M
P	E	A	C	O		U	T	H	O	R
O	F	F	L	I		R	A	R	Y	S
K	L	T	I	N		O	R	M	E	D
I	N	T	E	L		I	G	E	N	T
P	L	H	O	C		E	Y	N	E	V
A	T	T	R	E		U	A	L	O	F
B	A	C	C	O		P	L	I	S	H
P	I	N	D	U		T	R	Y	S	O
K	O	T	O	G		E	B	R	A	T
F	R	I	E	W		I	C	H	N	D
O	H	A	P	P		W	I	L	T	S
L	E	M	M	O		U	D	G	E	M
B	L	A	S	Q		O	W	E	L	S
O	M	A	N	A		E	R	Q	U	O

Name ______________________________ Date ____________________

216. More Analogies

Analogies are pairs of words with relationships. The first pair of words determines the relationship of the second pair of words. For example:

UP is to DOWN as IN is to __OUT__.

(UP is the opposite of DOWN; therefore, the proper analogy for IN is its opposite: OUT.) Fill in the blank with the analogous word based on the relationship established by the first pair of words.

1. FIVE is to TEN as FIFTEEN is to ____________________
2. WIN is to LOSE as BEGINNING is to ____________________
3. NOSE is to SMELL as EAR is to ____________________
4. I is to ME as HE is to ____________________
5. WEDNESDAY is to FRIDAY as JANUARY is to ____________________
6. B is to A as TEN is to ____________________
7. CAT is to MEOW as COW is to ____________________
8. FIVE is to E as TEN is to ____________________
9. BIRTH is to DEATH as DAWN is to ____________________
10. BEE is to HIVE as HUMAN is to ____________________
11. ROOM is to HOUSE as PETAL is to ____________________
12. BASEBALL is to BASEBALL PLAYER as PUCK is to ____________________
13. ICE is to SKATING as ____________________ is to SWIMMING
14. WEST is to LEFT as EAST is to ____________________
15. FISH is to SCHOOL as STUDENT is to ____________________

Name ______________________________ Date ____________________

217. Scrabble

Scrabble is a popular board game with a grid-like board and wooden letters. Each player has a group of letters. The players try to come up with words that connect to the words that are already on the board, or the players can extend words. For instance, if the word OX is on the board, a player can add EN to make OXEN. On the bottom right corner of each letter is a number. This number indicates the number of points the player gets for using that letter.

This activity is like the board game. Below is a board with two words. Underneath the board are your letters. Try to create as many words as you can horizontally or vertically by adding to the two words on the board. Remember, you may only use each letter once.

		N_1	O_1	R_1	T_1	H_4			
			P_3						
			E_1						
			N_1						

U_1	E_1	O_1	E_1	A_1
S_1	R_1	N_1	P_3	X_8

YOUR TOTAL SCORE: ______________________

Name ______________________________ Date ____________________

218. Circle Words

You will find at least 38 words in the letters around the circle. Some of the words are small words within bigger words. Move around from left to right and find as many words as you can. None of the words are scrambled. Write the words at the bottom of the page.

TELESCOPEWINDOWPOPCORNFRIENDSHIPINSECUREKIDNAPLANDFILLETTERHEADMAGNETNETWORKCHALKBOARDDOWNSTAIRSREPRESENT

Name ______________________________ Date ______________

219. More of Which Letter Comes Next?

The letters in a series follow a pattern. Determine the pattern and then add the next letter. For example: Aa Bb Cc Dd E e

1. A C E G I ____
2. A Z B Y C X ____
3. M N L O K P ____
4. A B D G K P ____
5. Z U P K ____
6. M N K L O P I J ____
7. F G H I J K L ____
8. S R Q P O N M ____
9. S I T T I S S I T T I ____
10. H H I J J K L L M N N ____

Name ______________________________ Date ____________________

220. Simon Says Some More

Do what Simon tells you to do.

Simon says . . . write down the name of the capital city of the U.S.A. ____________________

Simon says . . . drop the last three letters. ____________________

Simon says . . . change the first four letters to F I N D. ____________________

Simon says . . . drop the *ing* ending. ____________________

Simon says . . . change the "i" to "u." ____________________

Simon says . . . drop the last letter. ____________________

Simon says . . . change the "u" to "a." ____________________

Simon says . . . change the "n" to "r." ____________________

Simon says . . . add an "e" to the end of the word. ____________________

Simon says . . . add the word *well* to the end of the word. What have you got? ____________________

Name ______________________________ Date ____________________

221. It Takes Three Again

The words grouped below may appear to be unrelated. However, all the words belong in clusters of three beside the clues. Some words may fit in more than one cluster, so you may need to do some rearranging to make sure they all fit.

Iceland	Louisiana	Sigh	Connecticut	Dalmatian
Rottweiler	Carson City	Australia	Hyper	Arthur
Anger	Missouri	Wisconsin	Cry	Neil
Happy	Hawaii	Frankfort	St. Lawrence	Glad
Husky	New Zealand	Sad	Tennessee	Austria
Columbia	Die	Argentina	Heavy	Nile

1. Islands ______________________________
2. Types of dogs ______________________________
3. Descriptive words beginning with the letter "h" ______________________________
4. State capitals ______________________________
5. States ______________________________
6. Rivers ______________________________
7. Countries that begin with the letter "A" ______________________________
8. First name of famous American playwrights ______________________________
9. Three words that rhyme with each other ______________________________
10. Emotions ______________________________

Name ______________________________ Date ____________________

222. Person, Place, or Thing

The three clues in each case all point to a certain country that you need to identify. The clues include (1) the name of a famous person from that country; (2) the name of a major city in that country; and (3) the name of a famous event or object associated with that country. *Example:*

Person: Eleanor Roosevelt
Place: Washington
Thing: Rose Bowl Parade
Country: ***United States***

1. *Person:* Terry Fox
   Place: Halifax
   Thing: Calgary Stampede
   Country: ____________________

2. *Person:* Emperor Akhito
   Place: Yokohama
   Thing: Mount Fuji
   Country: ____________________

3. *Person:* Arten Senna
   Place: Sao Paulo
   Thing: Corpus Christi (statue)
   Country: ____________________

4. *Person:* Nelson Mandela
   Place: Johannesburg
   Thing: Voortrekker
   Country: ____________________

5. *Person:* Katarina Witt
   Place: Munich
   Thing: Oktoberfest
   Country: ____________________

6. *Person:* King Saud
   Place: Riyadh
   Thing: Oil
   Country: ____________________

7. *Person:* Leonardo da Vinci
   Place: Milan
   Thing: The Vatican
   Country: ____________________

8. *Person:* Anwar Sadat
   Place: Cairo
   Thing: The Sphinx
   Country: ____________________

9. *Person:* Paul Hogan
   Place: Canberra
   Thing: Ayers Rock
   Country: ____________________

10. *Person:* Indira Ghandi
    Place: Bombay
    Thing: Taj Mahal
    Country: ____________________

11. *Person:* Andrew Lloyd Weber
    Place: Brighton
    Thing: Wimbleton
    Country: ____________________

12. *Person:* Bjorn Borg
    Place: Goteburg
    Thing: The Gota Canal
    Country: ____________________

Name ________________________________ Date ____________________

223. The Code

You are attending the Private Investigator Institute. This is one of the final exam questions from your Breaking Codes 101 class. When you crack the code, you will reveal a message from a famous detective.

The only hints you have are the following:

= A   = B   = C

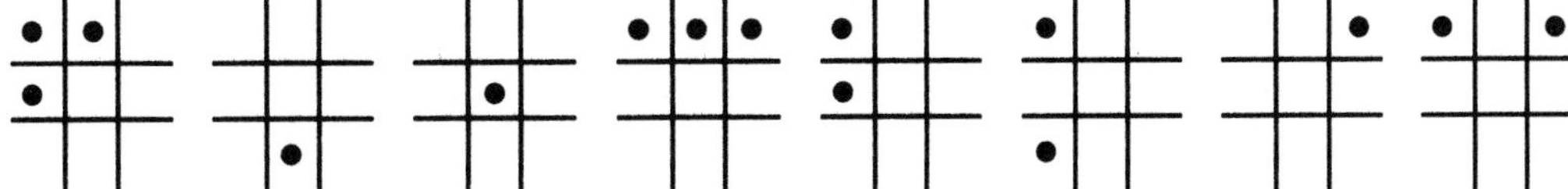

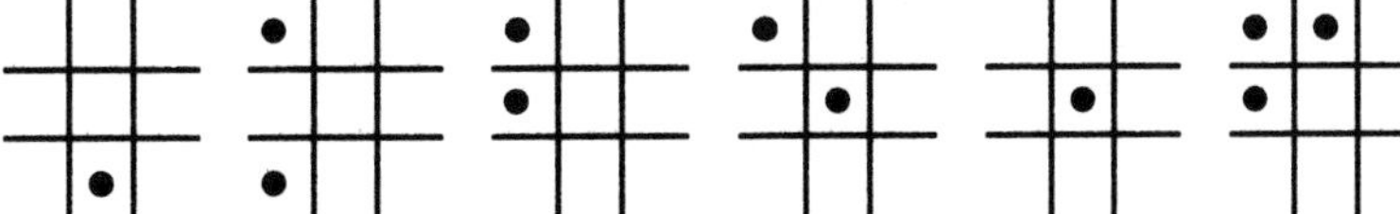

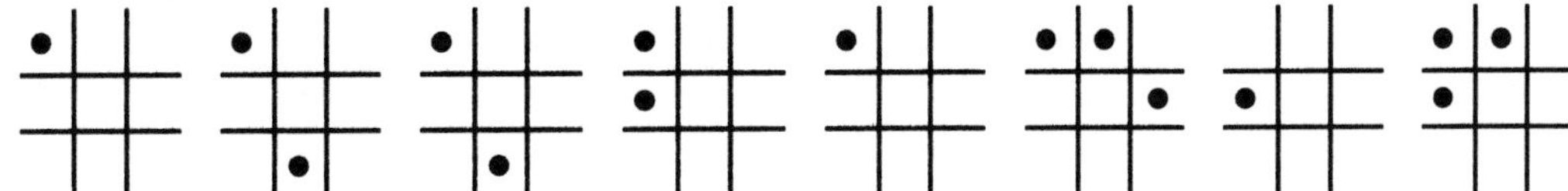

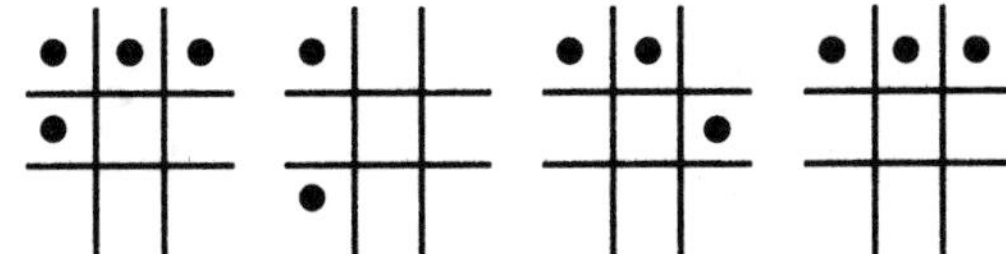

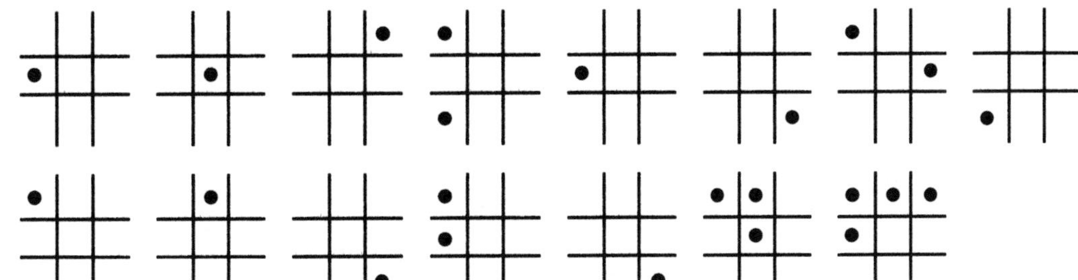

MESSAGE: ____

____

____

____

Name ________________________________ Date ____________________

224. MORE WORD CHANGES

Go from the word *BARN* to *MULE* by changing one letter at a time. Each time you change a letter, it must be a word.

BARN

____

____

____

MULE

Go from the word *HOPE* to *CATS* by changing one letter at a time. Each time you change a letter, it must be a word.

HOPE

____

____

____

CATS

Name ______________________________ Date ____________________

225. More Rhyming Pairs

Read the clues on the left-hand side to determine the rhyming pairs. Write the two words that rhyme—and also match the clues—on the lines. Example:

Medication for men named William ___Bill___ ___pill___

1. A mini shopping center ____________ ____________
2. What the coach gives players during half time ____________ ____________
3. The perfect group of athletes ____________ ____________
4. An enthusiastic royal female leader ____________ ____________
5. A courageous servant ____________ ____________
6. Yesterday moving quickly ____________ ____________
7. Colorless pottery ____________ ____________
8. When you can't wake up, this is what you're in ____________ ____________
9. Fairgrounds at night ____________ ____________
10. An activity to learn what people are called ____________ ____________
11. The color of the toboggan ____________ ____________
12. An actual feast ____________ ____________

ANSWER KEY

SECTION 1: LITERATURE

1–28. Answers will vary.

29. Magic Squares: Literary Terms

A 2	B 7	C 18	D 12
E 8	F 5	G 11	H 15
I 13	J 17	K 6	L 3
M 16	N 10	O 4	P 9

THE MAGIC NUMBER IS 39.

30. Timeline: A History of American Literature

5	3	6	8	1	2	7	9	4
(1770)	(1776)	(1789)	(1899)	(1917)	(1925)	(1930)	(1974)	(1993)

31. American Novelists and their Novels

3, 11, 8, 10, 1, 9, 5, 7, 13, 4, 15, 12, 14, 6, 2

32. Name That Author

Author #1—Mark Twain; Author #2—Stephen King; Author #3—Emily Dickinson

33. Famous English-Speaking Authors from Around the World

ACROSS: 2. Austen, 4. Twain, 5. Burnett, 6. Miller, 8. Atwood, 11. Conrad, 12. Spenser, 14. Lee, 15. Williams, 16. Montgomery, 18. Wilde, 19. Alcott; DOWN: 1. Hawthorne, 3. Salinger, 5. Bronte, 7. Hardy, 9. Orwell, 10. Dafoe, 12. Swift, 13. Shakespeare, 17. Dickens

34. Funny Titles

A–1 *The Cat in the Hat;* B–1 *Twelfth Night;* C–1 *The Prince and the Pauper;* A–2 *Fahrenheit 451;* B–2 *A Separate Peace;* C–2 *Cat on a Hot Tin Roof;* A–3 *Little Women;* B–3 *Brave New World;* C–3 *The Catcher in the Rye;* A–4 *The Cider House Rules;* B–4 *A Tale of Two Cities;* C–4 *The Grapes of Wrath*

SECTION 2: WRITING

35–36. Answers will vary.

37. Sentence Construction

(sample answers) 1. Arlene, a figure skater since age 3, wants to be an Olympic skater someday like her favorite skater Michelle Kwan. 2. Gerry's father Bud just got transferred

to Alaska from his company, New Wave Technology in Chapel Hill, North Carolina, but Gerry does not want to move.

38–66. Answers will vary.

SECTION 3: READING

67. Essay Introductions

Students should determine that introduction A is the better of the two introductions. Their reasons why will vary.

68. Answering the Famous Five

Who: six bulls; *What:* were stolen; *When:* last night; *Where:* Nebraska Big Rodeo; *How:* Someone smashed the gate open (the tire tracks near the pen indicate that the bulls were taken by truck).

69. Subjective or Objective

Sentence 1 ("The family . . .") Subjective; Sentence 2 ("Around midnight . . .") Objective; Sentence 3 ("Neither the . . .") Subjective; Sentence 4 ("It really isn't . . .") Objective; Sentence 5 ("Holy Cross . . .") Objective; Sentence 6 ("Some people . . .") Subjective; Sentence 7 ("Damage . . .") Objective; Sentence 8 ("Kennedy is . . .") Objective

70. Putting the News Story in Order

5, 4, 2, 7, 1, 6, 3

71. Todd's Wig

1. c; 2. c; 3. d; 4. b; 5. a; 6. a; 7. b; 8. b

72. Dear Mr. Twain

1. c; 2. d; 3. b; 4. b; 5. d

73. A Letter

1. an unborn baby; 2. October; 3. biting her nails; 4. none; 5. she eats right and bikes; 6. excited and nervous

74. Picnic Insects

1. b; 2. c; 3. d; 4. b; 5. a

75. Reading Ad Copy

1. a; 2. d; 3. b; 4. b; 5. b

76. E-Mails

1. Kelly is writing Kristy to tell her that Aunt Florence is not well and may die in the night; 2. 1 month old; 3. sisters; 4. work; 5. "Remember when she took us to Fenway Park in Boston for baseball games"; 6. letter or phone; 7. Kelly is at work and probably does not have a lot of time to spend e-mailing people; 8. Kristy heard the twins wake up from their nap.

77. Ingrid's Daytimer

1. She is taking the train to and from Chicago; 2. horseback riding; 3. The 11th is the best night because it's the only night that Ingrid is free; 4. Dave; 5. Answers will vary.

78. Classifieds

1. Answers will vary (People who like bargains. People who do not have a lot of money.); 2. in a local newspaper; 3. the writing is simple, direct, incomplete sentences, no unnecessary words; 4. Answers will vary. (The selling of these products won't generate enough money to justify the cost of advertising on TV or in a magazine); 5. The ad selling the Microwave, etc.; 6. 4

79. Subway Mania

1. Fisherhill; 2. Whitehorse, Buckingham, Bullhorn, and Buffalo; 3. Young; 4. Anderson; 5. six; 6. Park and Nadia

80. The Logic Puzzle

19. Kojimo; 20. Salt; 21. O'Connor; 22. Schwartz; 23. Dang; 24. Nguyen; 25. Dhaliwal; 26. Strahm

81. Traditional versus Modern

Answers will vary. (Students should notice that Cinderella is a more independent woman in the modern version, etc.)

82. Reading Poetry

1. "Don't weep for me at the last breath." (Reasons this is repeated may vary. For example, it may be repeated for emphasis.); 2. The author accepts death and thinks death will be positive; 3. Answers will vary; 4. Most lines from "Of free symphony concerts . . . will be cavity free" will be underlined; 5. Answers will vary.

83. Evaluating Endings

1–3. Answers will vary; 4. The actual ending is 2.

84. Dialogue

JEFF: I can't believe Aunt Sophie did it.

JEREMY: Did what?

JEFF: Got married.

UNCLE DAVID: Aunt Sophie got married!

JEREMY: When did this happen?

Jeff: On the weekend. Apparently she didn't tell any of us because she thought we'd try to talk her out of it.

UNCLE DAVID: Well, she's right. She's 80 years old. Jeff, don't you think she's a little too old to be getting married for the first time?

JEFF: No.

JEREMY: Yeah, what's wrong with it?

UNCLE DAVID: Because she's old enough to have a heart attack with all the excitement.

JEFF: Well, at least she'll die happy.

85. What Are They Doing?

1. star gazing; 2. tying a shoe; 3. lighting a fire; 4. playing Hide-and-Seek

86. What Is Being Described?

Answers will vary. However, this passage is written in such a manner that some students might think death is being described, while others might think birth is being described.

87. What Type of Story Is This?

This passage is a mystery. It is from *And Then There Were None* by Agatha Christie. There are various things that prove the passage is a mystery. The dialogue shows that the men are nervous (i.e., the reminder of making sure their doors are locked, etc.).

88. Describe the Shopper

The products from list 1 are from a healthy shopper. The products from list 2 are from a person who is less concerned with health. This shopper is probably very busy and not very healthy.

89. Directions

Dave's house

90. What Are They Saying?

Answers will vary.

91. More of What They Are Saying

Answers will vary.

92. A One-Minute Mystery

In order for a person to hang him-/herself, he/she could not stand on the chair and then kick it 14 feet. Thus, the crime scene is rather suspicious.

SECTION 4: GRAMMAR, PUNCTUATION, AND SENTENCE STRUCTURE

93. Parts-of-Speech Poem

noun, verb, noun, verb, adjectives, pronoun, conjunction, preposition, interjection, adverb

94. Parts of Speech: Analogies

1. mug; 2. Sacramento; 3. you; 4. green; 5. sing; 6. slowly; 7. on

95. Types of Nouns

PROPER NOUNS—Hoover Dam, Mr. Dhaliwal, Boston, North Dakota, Wednesday; COMMON NOUNS—house, football, dictionary, computer, friend; COLLECTIVE NOUNS—team, class, jury, committee, gang; ABSTRACT NOUNS—friendship, beauty, justice, love, afterthought

96. Collective Nouns

1. batch; 2. clump; 3. collection; 4. colony; 5. deck; 6. flock; 7. galaxy; 8. herd; 9. pack; 10. school

97. Pronoun Fun

1. a; 2. c; 3. b; 4. a; 5. b; 6. a

98. Pronoun Problems

x, √; x, √; √, x; x, √; √, x; x, √; √, x

99. Verb Tense

Answers will vary.

100. More on Verbs

1. b; 2. d; 3. b; 4. a; 5. b; 6. d

101. Irregular Verb Forms

ACROSS: 1. bled, 3. sang, 5. forbade, 6. ground, 7. went, 8. began, 9. brought, 11. did, 12. been, 14. known, 16. slept, 17. torn; DOWN: 1. build, 2. drank, 4. gotten, 5. forgotten, 8. beat, 9. been, 10. hidden, 12. burst, 13. eaten, 15. written, 18. run

102. Nouns, Adjectives, and Verbs

Answers will vary. Here are samples of a noun, adjective, and verb that may be used for each letter.

B—bat (noun), bright (adjective), bounce (verb)
M—mountain (noun), massive (adjective), move (verb)
S—sailboat (noun), scarlet (adjective), sink (verb)

103. Finding Subjects and Verbs

1. he; 2. read; 3. instructions; 4. paint; 5. can; 6. said; 7. he; 8. needed; 9. coats

Answer to the Riddle: He read the instructions on the paint can that said he needed two coats.

104. Sugject–Verb Agreement

1. sings; 2. is; 3. notices; 4. gives; 5. understand; 6. loves; 7. argues; 8. runs; 9. vote; 10. eats; 11. run; 12. breaks

The message: A SINGULAR subject needs a singular VERB.

105. A Sentence or Not a Sentence

This is a list of the song titles that are complete sentences:
"This House Is Not a Home"
"Go West"
"I Guess That's Why They Call It the Blues"
"I Wish I Felt Nothing"
"Raindrops Keep Falling on My Head"
"Help Me, Rhonda"

106. Book Titles and Sentence Fragments

Answers will vary.

107. Running Away with Run-on Sentences

The answer to the riddle is "Nowhere! Why would you bury survivors!"
Run-on sentences are 2, 3, 5, 6, 7, and 8.

108. Do-It-Yourself Sentences

Answers will vary.

109. Subjects, Predicates, and Objects

1. piece; 2. Tom, Randy; 3. swims laps at the pool every morning; 4. swims; 5. walked, talked; 6. a new Mercedes; 7. tickets; 8. me

110. More on Subjects, Predicates, and Objects

1. a; 2. d; 3. b; 4. c; 5. b; 6. a

111. Phrases, Clauses, and Conjunctions

1. Of all my friends; 2. I like you best; 3. We saw the Vietnam Memorial; 4. when we visited Washington; 5. when; 6. but; 7. of my friends

112. More on Phrases, Clauses, and Conjunctions

1. c; 2. a; 3. b; 4. d; 5. a

113. Types of Sentences

Answers will vary.

114. More About the Types of Sentences

Answers will vary.

115. Parallelism

1. Her car is powerful, fast, and inexpensive.
2. His career as a professional hockey player made him physically perfect, financially prosperous, and completely unhappy.
3. In the winter she wants to ski, but in the summer she likes to surf.
4. I want to go to the concert, but I am too poor, too busy, and too sick.
5. He likes his music loud, his food hot, and his bed made.

116. Misplaced Modifiers

√, x; √, x; x, √; √, x; x, √

117. Capitalization

1. While I was doing the laundry, Tammy called.
2. It is rather ironic that the Irish man speaks only Spanish.
3. When I go to the CN Tower in Toronto, I plan to go at Easter and try to visit my grandmother on Redmond Street.
4. On Saturday he leaves for Orlando.
5. They even have Heinz ketchup in Egypt.
6. Why did Admiral Leacock go to Kamsack, South Carolina?
7. Aunt Cindy is from Richmond, my uncle is from Ohio, and my friend Sandra is from the South.
8. Oh, I can't wait to visit Norway.
9. This Hindu speaks English.
10. I plan to visit Chicago with Elsie.

The answer to the riddle is "It is winter so he walks across on the ice."

118. Homophones

***	***	***
4	***	6
7	***	9
10	***	12
***	***	***

The correct homophones should be: 4. know; 6. They're; 7. to; 9. Where; 10. pair; 12. Whether

119. A Homophone Crossword

ACROSS: 1. steal, 3. whether, 4. patience, 8. reign, 10. ewe, 12. aisle, 13. mall, 15. need, 16. sighed, 17. their; DOWN: 1. scent, 2. ale, 4. peddle, 5. idle, 6. none, 7. earn, 9. guessed, 11. assent, 12. aunt, 13. minor, 14. lesson

120. Learning the Rules for Plurals

deer (10); beliefs (5); doors (1); videos (8); tomatoes (7); successes (2); cars (1); families (3); wives (6); cities (3); churches (2); sisters-in-law (9); heroes (7); moose (10); boys (4); wolves (6); patios (8); foxes (2)

121. Irregular Plurals

feet, teeth, indices, axes, bases, lice, oxen, children, women, species, media, foci, stimuli, crises, criteria, radii (or radiuses)

F	U	N	Y	I	J	I	C	O	F	M	W
S	E	A	H	Q	A	O	K	P	L	O	F
E	P	E	X	U	J	X	D	E	M	S	G
C	W	I	T	Z	N	E	E	E	T	P	I
I	V	S	E	B	C	N	N	S	O	E	L
D	U	K	E	H	L	I	C	E	I	C	U
N	M	R	T	S	F	R	N	S	I	I	M
I	C	G	H	Q	I	O	L	A	D	E	I
D	M	E	D	I	A	R	P	B	A	S	T
A	I	R	E	T	I	R	C	S	R	A	S
E	T	S	B	N	E	R	D	L	I	H	C

122. The Apostrophe: Contraction

Part One: 2. I'm; 3. you'll; 4. didn't; 5. it's; 6. who's; 7. we're; 8. couldn't; 9. he's; 10. aren't
Part Two: 2. isn't; 3. we've; 4. wouldn't; 5. it'll; 6. he'd; 7. can't; 8. you'll; 9. they're; 10. she's

123. The Apostrophe: Possession

Part One: 1. his; 2. Bryan's; 3. Christmas'; 4. bosses'; 5. women's; 6. woman's; 7. dogs'; 8. Chris's; 9. cities'; 10. their

Part Two: 1. My father's eldest sister's friend recently was appointed the United States' ambassador to China.

2. There are many bulls in the rodeo, but there are not enough bulls' pens.

3. In the sixties men's hair was much longer than in the fifties.

4. All of my friends' stresses revolve around final exams and the winter blahs.

5. I would rather go to Roman's house than to Margaret's.

124. Quotation Marks

***	2	3	4	5	***
7	***	9	10	***	12

(The shaded area should look like single quotation marks.)

2. In his anger, Carl asked me to fight him.
3. "A & P" is my favorite short story in a collection of short stories called *Pigeon Feathers* by John Updike.
4. Edger Allan Poe is a famous American poet who wrote a poem called "The Raven."
5. My favorite episode from the TV show *Friends* is called "The Triplets Arrive."
7. "When I write, I shake off all my cares," wrote Anne Frank in her diary.
9. Doug shouted, "Stop yelling, 'This is my day off.' I heard you the first time."
10. Otto asked, "Why did Janice leave?"
12. "I'm buying my first car next Friday," Mark said.

125. Punctuation Puzzle

1	***	3
4	***	6
7	***	9
10	11	12
13	***	15

(The shaded area is an exclamation mark.)

1. When are you going to the movie?
3. Raj, Stuart, Mary, Cam, and Sal talked in the cafeteria for the entire period.
4. Connor, who owns a store, recently filed for bankruptcy.
6. Mrs. Vijh has lived in Buffalo, New York her entire life.
7. She asked her friend when the party started.
9. The Canadians built the spaceship's engine; the Americans built the exterior.
10. She wanted to go to Caesar's Palace with you.
11. Did she attend the concert too?
12. Usually we go to the picnic as a family.
13. Are you going?
15. He said, "I realize that the American dollar is in a great position at the moment."

126. Punctuation Dot-to-Dot

The correct rules are 1, 3, 5, 6, 9, 10, 11, and 13.
The connected dots will make a fish.

The incorrect rules should be changed to:

2. Question marks are used at the end of direct questions.
4. A semicolon has the same function in a sentence as a period.
7. Semicolons are used to separate two independent clauses that do not have coordinating conjunctions between them.
8. A comma is sometimes used to introduce dialogue.
12. A comma separates three or more words in a series.

127. Punctuation Multiple-Choice

1. b; 2. c; 3. a; 4. b

128. You're the Editor

1. A; 2. D; 3. B; 4. E; 5. C; 6. F; 7. C; 8. G; 9. D; 10. E

Section 5: SPELLING

129. Able or Ible

1. able; 2. able; 3. ible; 4. ible; 5. able; 6. able; 7. ible; 8. able; 9. ible; 10. ible; 11. ible; 12. able; 13. ible; 14. able; 15. able; 16. ible; 17. able; 18. ible

130. Adding the Correct Letters

EI/IE: 1. weird; 2. deceive; 3. seize; 4. leisure; 5. caffeine; 6. niece; 7. wield; 8. ceiling; 9. receipt; 10. retrieve

ER/OR: 1. educator; 2. defender; 3. producer; 4. collector; 5. inspector; 6. inventor; 7. manager; 8. invader; 9. investigator; 10. visitor

ARY/ERY: 1. cemetery; 2. vocabulary; 3. January; 4. flattery; 5. boundary; 6. revolutionary; 7. elementary; 8. bakery; 9. library; 10. stationery; 11. stationary

131. What Is the Missing Vowel?

1. disappear; 2. college; 3. repetition; 4. business; 5. appreciate; 6. prejudice; 7. preparation; 8. irrelevant; 9. numerous; 10. together; 11. speech; 12. summary; 13. visible; 14. interest; 15. discussion; 16. boundary; 17. controversial; 18. satisfactory; 19. privilege; 20. innocent; 21. handkerchief; 22. obedience; 23. history; 24. ambition; 25. accurate; 26. salary; 27. separate; 28. sufficient; 29. skiing; 30. explanation

132. Computer Cards and Your Spelling Errors

Computers have a new program out now; it's called *Make-You're-Own-Cards.* It's a great idea except for one problem: spelling. There are lots of words that look like they are spelled correctly but they're actually not. Take, for example, the word *your.* Recently I received a personalized card that read: "You're the Greatest! Happy Birthday!" Then I received another personalized card that was signed "From your number one brother." At this point I knew there was a problem. Too many people use spellcheck on their computers but fail to proofread their cards. All the errors that I'm discussing would not be caught by spellcheck. It's not that I'm unappreciative of the cards sent to me; it's just that I'm concerned that people remember to check their spelling before the card is in its envelope and in the mail. Remember, you, too, can become a spelling master. All you need to do is edit your material.

133. Problem Words

1. except; 2. effect; 3. allowed; 4. are . . . our; 5. coarse; 6. dessert . . . desert; 7. farther; 8. latter; 9. forth . . . fourth; 10. peace . . . piece; 11. then . . . than; 12. role . . . roll

134. The Spelling Crossword

ACROSS: 1. controversy, 3. interrupt, 5. receive, 7. arctic, 9. victim, 10. February, 11. despair, 14. August, 16. adolescent, 18. thief, 19. sincerely; DOWN: 2. occurred, 4. mischief, 6. acquire, 7. amateur, 8. Indian, 12. eligible, 13. possess, 16. height, 17. terrible

135. The Spelling Bee

incorrect spelling: 3. prestige; 4. argument; 5. develop; 7. arrangement; 9. condemn; 10. occasion; 11.until; 12. stopped

The names of the students who made it to Round Two are Xavier, Seward, Brett, Veronica, Noelle, Ruth, Tristan, and Cole.

136. Spelling Activity

incorrect spelling: B. comfortable; C. unfortunately; F. preferred; H. prevalent; J. conceive; K. annually; L. apology; M. seize; O. tragic; P. fierce; Q. fascinate; S. schedule; T. miniature; U. February; V. especially; W. guilty; X. happened; Y. having; Z. picnicking

A good way to spend your leisure time: READING

137. Spelling Demons

1. acknowledgment; 2. hindrance; 3. supersede; 4. villain; 5. grammar; 6. representative; 7. embarrass; 8. precede; 9. exaggerate; 10. definitely; 11. calendar; 12. stubborn; 13. vegetable; 14. accommodate; 15. occasionally; 16. judgment

Note: Recent dictionaries are including *acknowledgement* as an acceptable spelling.

138. Which One Belongs?

(listed here is the corrected spelling) Group 1—cafeteria, laboratory, mathematics; Group 2—government, politician, professor; Group 3—continually, incredible, prepare; Group 4—absence, belief, courageous; Group 5—hundred, fourth, eighth; Group 6—maginary, knowledge, written; Group 7—paid, tried, preferred; Group 8—disastrous, extraordinary, magnificent

139. Spelling Maze I

******	******	professional	finally	obese	******
a lot	******	genius	impatient	******	******
visits	******	******	guarantee	******	luckily
victim	positive	******	which	******	approximate
committed	aggression	******	******	******	susceptible
negative	laziness	appearance	easier	unfortunately	embarrass
whether	receive	vegetate	intellectual	miscarriage	prescribe

140. Spelling Maze II

jealousy	favor	******	******	******	definitely
extremely	environment	******	vacuum	******	******
surprise	discipline	******	vengeance	sincerely	twelfth
******	******	******	absence	nonsense	receive
******	occurrence	courageous	benefited	awful	guidance
******	******	******	criticize	bulletin	running
skiing	writing	******	immediately	license	rhythm

141. Dot-to-Dot Spelling

The incorrect words are: 3. tries; 4. eligible; 10. really; 11. familiar; 14. pleasant; 17. performance; 18. generally.

The connected dots make a sailboat.

142. The Canadian Way

******	******	labor	******	check	******
******	traveling	counselor	******	center	******
******	******	defense	******	******	******
******	honor	leveled	******	neighbor	******
******	******	liter	******	favorite	******

The Canadian saying is "EH."

143. The Menu

Doug's, restaurant, appetizers, tomato, vegetable, Caesar, courses, kidney, fajitas, broccoli, casserole, parmesan, potatoes, lasagna, spaghetti, desserts, cinnamon, chocolate, beverages, coffee

144. The Job Application

1. Johnson & Johnson; 2. Proctor and Gamble; 3. General Motors; 4. Wal-Mart; 5. Hewlett-Packard; 6. Home Depot; 7. Texaco; 8. JC Penney; 9. Gillette; 10. McDonald's; 11. Allstate; 12. Metropolitan Life Insurance

145. Spelling States

Alabama, Alaska, Arizona, Arkansas, California, Colorado, Connecticut, Delaware, Florida, Georgia, Hawaii, Idaho, Illinois, Indiana, Iowa, Kansas, Kentucky, Louisiana, Maine, Maryland, Massachusetts, Michigan, Minnesota, Mississippi, Missouri, Montana, Nebraska, Nevada, New Hampshire, New Jersey, New Mexico, New York, North Carolina, North Dakota, Ohio, Oklahoma, Oregon, Pennsylvania, Rhode Island, South Carolina, South Dakota, Tennessee, Texas, Utah, Vermont, Virginia, Washington, West Virginia, Wisconsin, Wyoming

146. A+ Spelling Game

1. an; 2. ace; 3. ape; 4. ate; 5. ajar; 6. aunt; 7. acne; 8. admit; 9. argue; 10. alive; 11. awake; 12. August; 13. autumn; 14. auction; 15. algebra; 16. America; 17. anorexia; 18. alligator; 19. autograph; 20. anonymous

147. B+ Spelling Game

1. be; 2. boy; 3. buy; 4. belt; 5. blue; 6. bull; 7. bride; 8. blind; 9. banjo; 10. boxing; 11. branch; 12. bouquet; 13. brother; 14. bandage; 15. butcher; 16. biology; 17. bungalow; 18. birthday; 19. badminton; 20. beginning

148. Spelling Hexagon

Answers will vary. Here are some sample words that students can find: potato, pond, lend, tone, hat, dot, sat, hen, did, said.

149. The Spelling Box

Answers will vary. Here are some sample words that students can find: bee, best, pail, sip, money, grip, grass, lip, pass, sail, yes, no, at, song.

SECTION 6: VOCABULARY AND WORD BUILDING

150. Denotation and Connotation

The connotative definitions will vary. Here are some sample denotative definitions: Mother—a female parent; Home—a place where one lives; School—an institution for educating people; Love—a deep affection for a person; Television—a system that reproduces on screen a visual image and sound

151. Word Wheels

There are many possible combinations. Here are some of the words your students may create: contract, transcribe, transmit, confirm, action, acting, actor, design, designed, designing, firmly, transaction, distracted, retractable, signature.

152. Four-Letter Word Fun

There are many possible combinations. Here are some words your students may create: sand, tear, trap, deer, dear, mold, mole, pond, park, dome, stop.

153. Rhyming Wheels

Here are some possible words: ONE—stone, zone, bone, cone, tone, phone, alone, lone; ILL—still, will, pill, bill, mill, drill, fill, hill, grill, gill, frill; AIL—fail, hail, jail, mail, nail, bail, tail, wail, sail, frail; ELL—cell, bell, hell, shell, tell, spell, sell, well, smell; ING—bring, spring, thing, sting, sing, string, ring, king; AMP—tramp, cramp, camp, lamp, ramp, damp, champ, stamp

154. Creating "Sub" Words

Here are some possible words: subtitle, submarine, submission, subcontract, subhuman, sublease, substitute, subtropical, subterranean, subway, suburb, subscript.

155. Creating "Port" Words

Here are some possible words: portable, portage, portal, portcullis, portend, porter, portfolio, portico, portion, portrait, portray.

156. Word Pyramids

Here are some sample words for each pyramid: A—an, and, aunt, argue, attend; S—so, sew, sand, sting, string; T—to, two, trap, track, triple; D—do, did, dive, drive, device

157. Magic Squares: E Words

A 16	B 2	C 3	D 13
E 5	F 11	G 10	H 8
I 9	J 7	K 6	L 12
M 4	N 14	O 15	P 1

The Magic Number Is 34.

158. Improve Your Vocabulary

3, 9, 6, 11, 14, 10, 13, 5, 12, 2, 7, 8, 4, 15, 1

159. Multiple-Choice Vocabulary

1. b; 2. c; 3. a; 4. d; 5. a; 6. b

160. Other Words

(The meaning of these words is provided here.) 1. OCTOGENARIAN—an eighty-year-old; 2. FASTIDIOUS—very careful, fussily particular, meticulous; 3. MALEFACTORS—people who do evil; 4. THESPIAN—actor; 5. GENOCIDE—deliberate extermination of a people or nation; 6. GRANDIOSE—producing an imposing effect; 7. ILLUMINATING—enlighten intellectually; 8. JUVENESCENCE—youthful; 9. NEFARIOUS—wicked; 10. INTROVERT—reserved, shy

161. A Letter

(The meaning of the words in bold is provided here.) AUSPICIOUS—favorable; FELICITATIONS—congratulations; VENERABLE—deserving profound respect on account of age; PRODIGIOUS—marvelous, enormous; RETROSPECT—reference to a past time; ARDENT—eager, passionate; ABUNDANCE—plenty; CONSEQUENCE—importance; ADORING—regard with deep affection; COMMEMORATE—be a memorial to; PONDER—think over, consider; ENCROACH—intrude; SUBSCRIBE—contribute, pay

162. An Antonym Box

ACROSS: 1. exterior, 2. right, 3. thankful, 9. left, 10. horizontal, 11. death, 12. end; DOWN: 1. earliness, 4. light, 5. thin, 6. new, 7. winner, 8. reject, 13. hate, 14. high, 15. smooth

163. Another Antonym Box

ACROSS: 1. inside, 2. evil, 3. left, 4. true, 10. lose, 11. tall, 12. night, 13. learn; DOWN: 1. in, 5. end, 6. down, 7. north, 8. hot, 9. tame, 14. tail, 15. exit, 16. rare, 17. over, 18. no

164. The Synonym Chart

(Answers will vary. Here are some suggested synonyms.) WALK—stroll, saunter, hike; MONEY—cash, coin, funds; GOOD—excellent, great, beneficial; BEGINNING—start, debut, opening; GOVERNMENT—administration, regime, ruler; THANKFUL—grateful, appreciative, obliged; MUSIC—tune, melody, score; RAIN—shower, downpour, drizzle; COLD—frosty, frigid, chilly; LIGHT—beam, ray, shimmer; TALK—speak, converse, chat; TEST—quiz, exam, trial; RICH—wealthy, affluent, opulent; SLEEP—nap, rest, slumber; PRISON—jail, cell, penitentiary; STOP—suspend, halt, cease; MOUNTAIN—hill, peak, elevation; LANGUAGE—speech, dialect, jargon; POOR—penniless, beggary, broke; VACATION—trip, journey, excursion

165. A Synonym Box

ACROSS: 1. small, 2. lethal, 3. liberation, 9. expire, 10. novice, 11. excursion; DOWN: 1. snare, 4. nuisance, 5. exit, 6. too, 7. odd, 8. dawdle, 12. temple, 13. silent, 14. yes, 15. envy

166. Another Synonym Box

ACROSS: 1. rainstorm, 2. movie, 3. earth, 4. hat, 10. hop, 11. rich, 12. fear, 13. elf, 14. lake, 15. evil, 16. pie; DOWN: 1. relative, 5. trench, 6. hotel, 7. lawn, 8. nation, 9. nap, 17. tap, 18. light, 19. devil, 20. end

167. Career Jargon

1. a; 2. a; 3. b; 4. c; 5. a; 6. c; 7. b; 8. a; 9. c; 10. b

168. Ology Vocabulary

Anthropology (human—culture); Archaeology (ancient people); Cardiology (heart); Etymology (word origins); Geology (earth); Gynecology (women); Herpetology (reptiles); Meteorology (weather); Neurology (nerves—the nervous system); Ornithology (birds); Paleontology (fossils); Pomology (fruit); Psychology (mind); Seismology (earthquakes); Theology (God); Zoology (animals)

169. What Do They Fear?

Aerophobia (flying); Arachnophobia (spiders); Brontophobia (thunder); Claustrophobia (closed spaces); Cynophobia (dogs); Gerontophobia (old age); Hemophobia (blood); Mikrophobia (germs); Murophobia (mice); Numerophobia (numbers); Ophidiophobia (snakes); Phonophobia (speaking aloud); Thaasophobia (being bored); Triskaidekaphobia (number 13); Xenophobia (strangers)

170. Which Word Doesn't Belong? (Part I)

1. taciturn; 2. impeccable; 3. benevolent; 4. cooperation; 5. veracity; 6. certitude; 7. scrupulous; 8. illustrious; 9. tenancy

171. Which Word Doesn't Belong? (Part II)

1. aroma; 2. feign; 3. transmogrify; 4. titan; 5. gregarious; 6. impecunious; 7. fissure; 8. impermeable; 9. prurient

172. Which Word Doesn't Belong? (Part III)

1. submissive; 2. hard-shell; 3. nonentity; 4. assent; 5. maudlin; 6. arcane; 7. postulant; 8. ambivalent; 9. unflappable

Section 7: LISTENING AND SPEAKING SKILLS

173–187. Answers will vary.

188. Listening Skills Quiz

1. false; 2. true; 3. true; 4. false; 5. true; 6. true; 7. true; 8. false; 9. true; 10. true; 11. true; 12. true

189. The Substitute Teacher's Day

(Bookcase)

(pencil sharpener)

Mary Little	Rory Mackenzie	Caroline Carson	
Carrie Sloan	Cory Mackenzie	Jerry Bond	(window)
Joel Ford	Kevin Taylor	Ashley Anderson	
Adam Walker			

190. The Shopping Trip

(to the subway)	Coffee Time	
The Daily Grill		
	Hall's Drugstore	
McDonald's		
	The Bombay Company	The Body Shop
Payless Shoes		
Fairweather		
Jean Machine	Holt Renfrew	
(news stand)		

191. The Listening Grid

	1	2	3	4	5	6	7	8	9	10	11	12	13	14	15	16	17	18	19	20
1																				
2										*										
3									*		*									
4								*				*								
5									*		*									
6								*				*								
7							*						*							
8								*				*								
9							*						*							
10						*								*						
11					*	*	*	*	*	*	*	*	*	*	*					
12									*		*									
13									*		*									
14							*	*	*	*	*	*	*	*						
15						*									*					
16			*	*	*											*	*	*		
17	*	*																	*	*

When you have finished, you will have drawn an evergreen tree.

192. What's Missing?

dream; right; jigged; llama; beach; hare; brother; neighbor's; father; barked; tonight; dreams

193. A Listening Poem

1. A Day at the Office; 2. the principle cellist; 3. his arms; 4. the tuba player's drinking habits, the clarinetist's wife's awful cooking, the difficulty in toilet training a two-year-old; 5. with his chins; 6. no number is given, but it is a full house; 7. flute, double bass, cello, violin, tuba, and clarinet

SECTION 8: WORD FUN

194. Which Letter Comes Next?

1. T; 2. T; 3. E; 4. A; 5. K; 6. V; 7. Y; 8. X; 9. O; 10. N

195. Simon Says

beverage; rage; page; plate; late; later; latter; batter; bat; cat; category

196. A Simile Snake

1. cut; 2. thumb; 3. bird; 4. dog; 5. grass; 6. sandpaper; 7. rail; 8. lamb; 9. bee; 10. elephant; 11. taxes; 12. shop; 13. pig; 14. glove; 15. eagle; 16. eel; 17. log

197. A Palindrome Letter

MOM; DAD; WOW; DID; EVE; NOON; KAYAK; POP; BOB; GAG; TOT; BOB; EYE; SIS; OTTO

198. Word Chains

Answers will vary. Here are some sample answers.

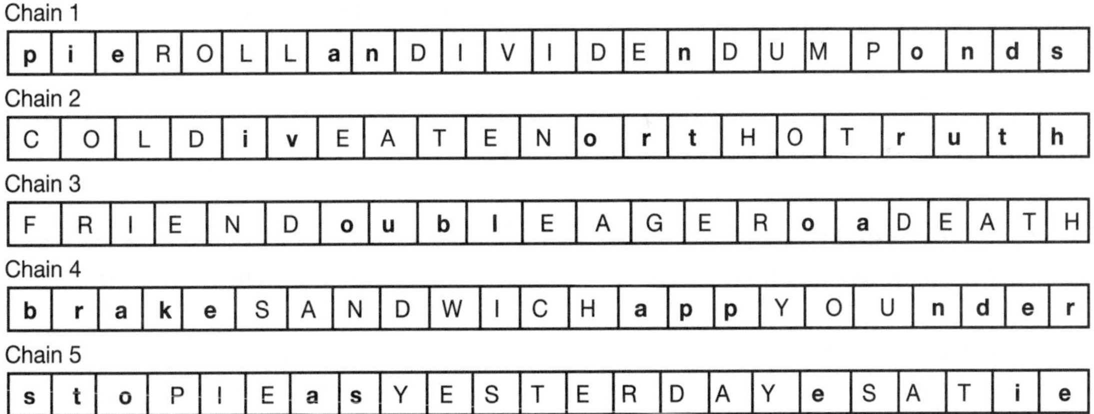

Chain 1
p i e R O L L a n D I V I D E n D U M P o n d s
Chain 2
C O L D i v E A T E N o r t H O T r u t h
Chain 3
F R I E N D o u b l E A G E R o a D E A T H
Chain 4
b r a k e S A N D W I C H a p p Y O U n d e r
Chain 5
s t o P I E a s Y E S T E R D A Y e S A T i e

199. It Takes Three

1. New York, South Carolina, Hawaii; 2. Toyota, Ford, Honda; 3. Virginia, Georgia, Alexandra; 4. Saturn, Venus, Pluto; 5. Nile, Amazon, Mississippi; 6. hills, mountains, cliffs; 7. Canada, Russia, Alaska; 8. star, airplane, bird; 9. Clinton, Lincoln, Washington; 10. Boston, Dallas, Denver

200. Career Alphabet

Answers will vary. Here are some samples: Acupuncturist; Butcher; Chef; Dentist; Electrician; Farmer; Gynecologist; Hairdresser; Insurance Salesperson; Jockey; Karate Instructor; Lawyer; Minister; Nurse; Optometrist; Police Officer; Quilt Maker; Radio Disc Jockey; Secretary; Teacher; Undertaker; Veterinarian; Waitress; X-ray Technician; Youth Worker; Zoologist

201. Word Removal

The message reads TREAT EVERYONE WITH RESPECT.

202. Analogies

1. right; 2. nest; 3. ten; 4. June; 5. pack; 6. football player/hockey player (a few answers are acceptable here); 7. ride/peddle; 8. principal; 9. three; 10. yellow; 11. morning; 12. dive; 13. lose; 14. seven; 13. bug/insect; 16. adult/teenager; 17. south; 18. green

203. School Scramble

1. geography; 2. student; 3. chalk; 4. atlas; 5. classroom; 6. principal; 7. binder; 8. examination; 9. textbook; 10. cafeteria; 11. pencil; 12. mathematics

204. Word Building

Answers will vary.

205. Alphabet Soup

togEther; frieNdship; fiXed; banAna; remeMber; vegeTable; horrIble; Before; fatheR; damaGe; craZy; fiCtion; finisH; Famous; Quiet; braVe; happY; steaK; obviOus; marveLous; unprePared; senSation; Wealth; Jolly; stuDent; ambUlance

206. Word Changes

Talk to Tale to Sale to Sole to *Sold*
Dove to Love to Live to Life to *Lift*

207. Unsolved Mysteries

If you solve this mystery, you may want to consider a career as a private investigator.

208. Rhyming Pairs

1. double trouble; 2. tin bin; 3. top cop; 4. mop shop; 5. foe Joe; 6. smog fog; 7. spring fling; 8. sold gold; 9. dry eye; 10. fall ball; 11. down clown; 12. bride cried

209. What Is the Mystery Word

science; Christmas; look; apple; blush

210. Letter Math

1. mother; 2. height; 3. nobody; 4. coffee; 5. monkey; 6. engine; 7. lumber; 8. orange; 9. dollar; 10. strong; 11. driver; 12. bottom

211. Another Word Removal

The message reads EAT LOTS OF VEGETABLES.

212. Going on a Camping Trip

The trick is that the students only can take items that have double letters in them (like haMMer, paDDle, bOOk, etc). That is why they can take an apple, but not an orange. The students' lists will vary. The only correct lists will have items with double letters.

213. What's the Word?

A–1 coffee break; B–1 high school; C–1 rocking chair; D–1 square dance; E–1 downtown; A–2 hole in one; B–2 six feet underground; C–2 time flies; D–2 tea for two; E–2 mixed doubles; A–3 eyeball; B–3 fork in the road; C–3 bookmark; D–3 three-part harmony; E–3 the plot thickens; A–4 sleeping on the job; B–4 railway crossing; C–4 wear your heart on your sleeve; D–4 mood swings; E–4 up the creek without a paddle; A–5 double trouble; B–5 I will get around to it; C–5 two-car garage; D–5 drug overdose; E–5 left out

214. Letter Pairs

1. ambulances; 2. propaganda; 3. wonderland; 4. cheesecake; 5. salutation; 6. housewives; 7. woodpecker; 8. dictionary; 9. respirator; 10. triumphant

215. More Alphabet Soup

bRother; arTicles; introDuce; Campus; versiOn; desigN; cEntury; fleXible; busIness; Using; apProach; Wrong; Author; liBrary; inForm; intelLigent; hocKey; eQual; accoMplish; induStry; Zebra; wHich; happY; Judge; Vowel; manaGer

216. More Analogies

1. thirty; 2. end; 3. hear; 4. him; 5. March; 6. nine; 7. moo; 8. J; 9. sunset (or dusk); 10. house; 11. flower; 12. hockey player; 13. water; 14. right; 15. class

217. Scrabble

Answers will vary.

218. Circle Words

friend, end, ship, friendship, in, secure, insecure, cure, kid, nap, kidnap, land, fill, landfill, ill, let, letter, head, letterhead, magnet, net, network, work, chalk, board, chalkboard, down, own, stairs, downstairs, represent, present, sent, telescope, scope, window, win, wind, pop, corn, popcorn

219. More of Which Letter Comes Next?

1. K; 2. D; 3. J; 4. V; 5. F; 6. Q; 7. M; 8. L; 9. S; 10. O

220. Simon Says Some More

Washington; washing; finding; find; fund; fun; fan; far; fare; farewell

221. It Takes Three Again

1. Hawaii, New Zealand, Iceland; 2. Dalmatian, Husky, Rottweiler; 3. hyper, heavy, happy; 4. Frankfort, Carson City, Columbia; 5. Connecticut, Louisiana, Wisconsin; 6. Missouri, St. Lawrence, Nile; 7. Austria, Australia, Argentina; 8. Neil, Arthur, Tennessee; 9. cry, sigh, die; 10. sad, glad, anger

222. Person, Place, or Thing

1. Canada; 2. Japan; 3. Brazil; 4. South Africa; 5. Germany; 6. Saudi Arabia; 7. Italy; 8. Egypt; 9. Australia; 10. India; 11. Britain; 12. Sweden

223. The Code

Sherlock Holmes applauds your decoding ability.

224. More Word Changes

Barn to Bare to Bale to Male to *Mule*
Hope to Cope to Cops to Cots to *Cats*

225. More Rhyming Pairs

1. small mall; 2. chalk talk; 3. dream team; 4. keen queen; 5. brave slave; 6. fast past; 7. gray clay; 8. deep sleep; 9. dark park; 10. name game; 11. red sled; 12. real meal